30-MINUTE CAST-IRON COOKBOOK

30-MINUTE
CAST-IRON
COOKBOOK

80 Fast, Everyday Recipes for Your Favorite Skillet

ROBIN DONOVAN

PHOTOGRAPHY BY DARREN MUIR

ROCKRIDGE
PRESS

For general information on our other products and services or to obtain technical support, please contact our Customer Care Department within the United States at (866) 744-2665, or outside the United States at (510) 253-0500.

Rockridge Press publishes its books in a variety of electronic and print formats. Some content that appears in print may not be available in electronic books, and vice versa.

Interior and Cover Designer: Diana Haas
Art Producer: Meg Baggott
Editor: Annie Choi
Production Editor: Ruth Sakata Corley
Production Manager: Riley Hoffman

Photography © 2021 Darren Muir. Food styling by Yolanda Muir

Cover: Steak Fajitas, page 105

ISBN: Print 978-1-63807-922-4 | eBook 978-1-63807-551-6
R0

Contents

Introduction

"What should I cook?" If you're anything like me, this is a question you ask yourself multiple times a day, every single day. I love to cook, and I'm pretty dang good at it, but I still get tired of having to cook so many meals. And yet, my family expects to eat several meals a day (the nerve!). My solution has been to hone lots of quick, easy-to-prepare recipes. In doing so, I've come to love an unlikely piece of cookware— my trusty cast-iron skillet.

I know what you're thinking. "Isn't cast iron only good for heavy, long-cooking dishes? And isn't it really hard to clean and maintain?" Or "Won't it make my life more difficult instead of easier?" The answer to all these questions is a resounding, "Nope!"

It's true that cast-iron skillets are the ideal cooking vessels for many long-cooked recipes, like stews and braises, and heavy, once-in-a-while indulgences, like baked mac and cheese, with its crispy, golden-brown topping, or buttery, dense corn bread. But cast iron is also great for quick-cooking methods—stir-frying, sautéing, searing, and roasting—thanks to its unparalleled ability to retain heat.

These days, I use my cast-iron skillet most often for quick dishes like eggs, pancakes, seared meat and fish, fried chicken, or stir-fried vegetables. The skillet is also great for quick bakes—flaky biscuits, nachos, and fruit crisps.

If you've never used cast-iron cookware before, I get that it might seem a little intimidating. It is true that cast-iron cookware requires different treatment than nonstick, stainless-steel, or enameled cookware. But the truth is that caring for cast iron is easy. This book will show you, in detail, everything you need to know about seasoning, cleaning, and storing your skillet so that it's always ready to go when you are. I promise that once you learn the basics, cleaning and caring for your cast-iron skillet isn't time-consuming or arduous in the least.

As a professional cookbook author and recipe developer, I've got a well-equipped kitchen with some pretty fancy cookware, but I still hold my old, inexpensive cast-iron pans in the highest regard. They've earned themselves an honored place in my kitchen—front and center, ready to be put to use on a daily basis—for long-cooking dishes as well as 30-minute meals. They're so incredibly versatile that I can't imagine cooking day to day without them. And I'm confident that even if you don't already, you'll soon feel the same way about your cast-iron pan.

Whether you're new to cooking in cast iron or a "seasoned" cast-iron cook looking for new recipes, this book is full of ideas for cast-iron skillet dishes that can be on the table in 30 minutes or less (and that includes the prep time!). Recipes range from breakfast and brunch, simple sides, snacks, and desserts to vegetarian, meat, poultry, and fish and seafood-based main dishes—you're sure to find plenty of fast and easy options to put your skillet to work and a tasty, satisfying meal on the table.

CHAPTER 1

A SKILLET MADE FOR EVERY DAY

If you're looking for a single piece of cookware that can take you from breakfast to a late-night dessert, you've come to the right place. With a good cast-iron skillet and a handful of ingredients, you can be just minutes away from a delicious, nutritious meal—any time of day. This chapter will tell you everything you need to know to make the most of your cast-iron skillet, every day.

Cast Iron and . . .
Fast, Everyday Cooking?

Because you picked up this book, I'm guessing that you want to use your cast-iron skillet more often. There's a common misconception that cast-iron cookware is only good for long-cooking dishes or baked goods, but the truth is that a cast-iron skillet is an ideal piece of equipment for fast, everyday cooking, too.

Sure, your mother or grandmother probably used her cast-iron cookware to make lots of comfort food dishes, like mac and cheese, chili, and fried chicken, so you may think that cast-iron cookware is made exclusively for heavy and time-consuming dishes. And you may have fallen prey to the myth that cast iron is difficult to clean and care for. But keep reading and you'll discover that neither of these beliefs is true.

This book will prove to you once and for all that a cast-iron skillet is super versatile and just as useful for making light and quick-cooking dishes as it is for Grandma's indulgent specialties. It will also demystify the process of cleaning and caring for cast-iron cookware. Trust me, it is much easier than you think.

When you've got the right tools and you know how to use them, cooking good, homemade meals from scratch becomes a source of joy rather than a chore. Confidence comes from understanding how your tools work and learning the skills needed to use those tools to their full potential.

In this book, you'll find everything you need to know to wield your cast-iron skillet like a pro, as well as 80 recipes for dishes you can make in your trusty cast-iron skillet in 30 minutes or less.

Cast-iron cookware's list of advantages is long. At the top of that list is superior heat conduction. Iron can be heated to very high temperatures, and it conducts heat better than any other cooking material; the heat carries through the entire surface of the pan without any hot or cold spots. The high heat it can take and superior heat conduction of cast iron make it the perfect surface for quick-cooking dishes.

Cast iron not only gets extremely hot, it also retains that heat, even when you add cold foods to the pan. Add a thick steak to a stainless-steel or nonstick-coated aluminum skillet, and the skillet's temperature drops. As the temperature comes back up, the food cooks, but it doesn't create that hard sear you want. You can get that hard sear with cast iron.

History of the
Cast-Iron Skillet

Cast-iron cookware has a long and storied history that goes as far back as the Han Dynasty (206 BCE to 220 CE). Its first appearance on American soil dates back as far as 1619.

According to historians, George Washington's mother included instructions for distributing her cast-iron cookware in her will in 1788. And explorers Lewis and Clark are believed to have carried Dutch ovens made of cast iron on their Louisiana Territory expedition in the early 19th century.

In those early years, American cast-iron cooking pots were designed to stand on legs or hang from hooks over an open fire. They were redesigned to feature flat bottoms once the indoor cooking stove came on the scene in the late 18th century. And in fact, virtually all cooking pots used in the United States were made of cast iron until around the middle of the 20th century. It wasn't until after World War II, when arms factories were drowning in surpluses of stainless steel and aluminum, that these lighter-weight types of cookware appeared. And in the 1960s, Teflon was introduced as a nonstick coating for aluminum or steel pans, increasing their popularity.

While lightweight, nonstick cookware surged in popularity, cast-iron pots and pans lived on in people's kitchens. Because of their durability, they continued to be passed from one generation to the next.

Once the pride of grandmothers and antique cookware collectors, cast-iron cookware is experiencing a significant resurgence in popularity. Younger home cooks are seeking out cast-iron cookware. Some may be tired of having to replace less-durable forms of cookware over and over again. Concern over the leaching of toxic chemicals from nonstick coatings may motivate others. And some may simply appreciate the fact that cast iron is one of the best materials for cooking.

In a cast-iron skillet, the outside of a food can be seared quickly, which locks in the juices and flavors and caramelizes the food's surface, giving it great depth of flavor.

A cast-iron skillet works wonders with quick stovetop dishes like griddled pancakes, fried eggs, crispy-on-the-outside-gooey-on-the-inside grilled cheese sandwiches, deep-fried fritters, and quick stir-fries.

When properly seasoned (see page 9), a cast-iron skillet provides an all-natural nonstick cooking surface. You don't have to worry about food sticking to the pan or waste time scraping off cooked-on food.

For all these reasons, cast-iron cooking is the ideal method to choose for quick meals. Whether you're searing steaks; stir-frying vegetables; baking casseroles; or roasting meat, poultry, or potatoes, you can count on your sturdy cast-iron skillet for high-heat, nonstick cooking.

Methods for Quick-Cooking in Cast Iron

Cast-iron skillets are extremely versatile. They can be used to cook everything from a quickly fried egg to a slowly braised stew or baked biscuits. But because this book is all about recipes that can be cooked in cast iron in 30 minutes or less, I'm going to focus on quick-cook methods such as searing, sautéing, and stir-frying.

SEAR

Thanks to its ability to maintain high, even heat, a cast-iron skillet is perfect for searing everything from steaks or chicken thighs to vegetables such as Brussels sprouts or green beans. In order to get a good sear, you want to get the pan very hot before placing ingredients in it. Put the ingredients in the hot pan and cook until the bottom side is nicely browned. Flip the food and do the same on the other side. Searing can be accomplished in just a few minutes, but some foods will need to be finished in the oven or another way in order to be fully cooked through. See the recipes for Fish Tacos with Cilantro Lime Slaw (page 74), Seared Scallops with Peas and Bacon (page 76), Pan-Seared Chicken with Brussels Sprouts, Bacon, and Apples (page 90), and Seared Flank Steak Salad with Warm Balsamic-Bacon Vinaigrette (page 100) for examples.

SAUTÉ AND STIR-FRY

Thanks to its even heat and nonstick surface, a cast-iron skillet is great for sautéing and stir-frying foods. Always use plenty of fat. Because of its ability to get very, very hot, a cast-iron skillet can function very much like a wok for stir-frying meat or vegetables that have been cut into small pieces. See Blistered Green Beans with Shallots (page 41), Stir-Fried Rice Noodles with Tofu and Broccoli (page 58), Spicy Stir-Fried Kung Pao Shrimp (page 78), and Steak Fajitas (page 105).

DEEP-FRY

Deep-frying refers to cooking food in a pan filled with fat (oil, butter, lard, etc.) that has been heated to high temperature. Food is dropped into the hot fat and cooks quickly, giving it a golden-brown, crisp outer crust. See Corn Fritters (page 38), Shrimp Po' Boy Sandwiches (page 80), and Crispy Fried Chicken Strips (page 87).

BAKE, ROAST, AND BROIL

Baking, roasting, and broiling are done with dry heat in the oven instead of on the stovetop. Baking is cooking something in an oven at a moderate temperature, 300°F to 350°F. Casseroles, breads, and desserts are example of baked foods. Roasting relies on high temperatures (350°F or above) and is ideal for cooking large cuts of tender meat, fish, and vegetables. Broiling uses only the broiler function in an oven set at high heat to quickly brown the top of food.

Baking and roasting are often used for longer-cooking dishes, but all three of these cooking methods can be used to quickly cook dishes like pizza, fish, or chicken, or to finish dishes that are started on the stovetop. For instance, steak is often quickly seared on the stovetop and finished in the oven at a moderate or high temperature. And many dishes can be run under the broiler just before serving to brown and crisp the top or melt a layer of cheese. See Glazed Cinnamon Skillet Cake (page 24), Skillet-Roasted Feta and Tomatoes with Pasta (page 56), and Pumpkin Mac and Cheese (page 54).

BRAISE AND STEW

Braising is a cooking process that uses low, wet heat. To braise foods, you bring a small amount of liquid—broth, wine, water, or other liquids all work—to a simmer. Add the ingredients, cover, and cook over medium heat (usually 300°F or 350°F) on the stovetop or in the oven. It is an ideal cooking method for large cuts of meat because it infuses the meat with flavor while keeping it tender and moist. For instance, a beef stew is cooked by braising. This method is especially well suited to cooking inexpensive cuts of meat (think pork butt, brisket, or stew meat) that can start out tough but become tender through the braising process. Although many braised dishes must cook for long periods of time, when you use quicker-cooking ingredients, like fish, chicken, or vegetables, they can be cooked much more quickly. Cast-iron skillets are perfect for this type of braising because they heat quickly and hold the heat so well. See Chicken Chile Verde (page 93) and Beef and Sweet Potatoes in Thai Curry Sauce with Coconut Milk (page 99).

The Properties of the Pan

Cast-iron cookware comes in many different shapes and sizes. It also comes unseasoned and uncoated, uncoated and preseasoned, or enameled. Each of these attributes lends itself to different styles of cooking and uses, so it's a good idea to consider these factors before purchasing a cast-iron skillet, if you don't have one already. Following you'll find an explanation of how each attribute affects performance and care requirements.

SIZE AND WEIGHT

Cast-iron pots come in many shapes and sizes, from teeny, tiny decorative skillets to medium-size griddles, ridged grill pans, and industrial-size Dutch ovens. Griddles, of course, are great for cooking things such as pancakes; grill pans are terrific for mimicking a grilled effect when cooking indoors on your stovetop; and Dutch ovens can be used to cook stews, soups, and chilis. This book focuses on recipes using a skillet, so although you may want to expand your collection to include various other cookware pieces, you'll only need a skillet to make the recipes here.

One thing to keep in mind when selecting cast-iron cookware pieces is their weight. Cast iron is by nature quite heavy. Larger pieces will obviously be heavier than smaller pieces. This may not seem like a big deal at first glance, but try tilting eggs around a 14-inch cast-iron skillet to make a thin, delicate omelet, and you'll quickly realize why a smaller pan might be a good idea.

In this book, we focus on a basic, medium-size cast-iron skillet. I find that a 12-inch skillet is the best starter piece. It's large enough for most recipes but not so large that it is unwieldy. The recipes in this book are all written for a 12-inch skillet, although a 10- or 14-inch skillet will also work for most of the recipes.

In recent years, several companies have begun using new manufacturing techniques to produce lighter-weight cast-iron cookware that still delivers the performance benefits of the classic pieces. For a typical medium-size skillet, the difference in weight can be as much as two or three pounds. These lighter-weight pieces still do a good job of conducting and retaining heat, but you may find that they don't do it quite as well as the traditional heavy stuff.

SURFACE TREATMENT

Another factor to consider is the surface of the pan. Traditional cast-iron pans are made of uncoated metal that must be seasoned. These days you can buy uncoated cast-iron pans that come preseasoned. There are also cast-iron pans that are coated with a vitreous enamel glaze.

Some argue that uncoated cast iron provides a better sear and is therefore superior for cooking meats and other ingredients that require a hard sear. Uncoated cast iron is also extremely affordable and very, very durable.

Enameled cast-iron pans have a few advantages over bare cast iron. Chief among these is that enameled pans are naturally nonstick and do not need to be seasoned. Many find they are also easier to clean and care for. In addition, uncoated pans can leach iron when they are used to cook acidic foods such as tomatoes, giving the food an unpleasant metallic flavor, whereas coated pans can be used for any type of food, regardless of acidity. Many cooks also appreciate enameled pans for the fact that they come in a rainbow of pretty colors, in contrast to the matte black of an uncoated cast-iron pan.

The disadvantages of enameled pans are that they are significantly more expensive and somewhat less durable—the enamel can eventually become scratched, which reduces the pan's "nonstickiness" and eventually can lead to deterioration of the iron underneath.

Both enameled and uncoated cast-iron cookware is oven-safe, usually up to at least 500°F. Do note, however, that some pans have handles made from materials that are not as heat-resistant, so be sure to check the manufacturer's guidelines about oven-safeness and maximum temperature. Ideally, you'll want to choose a pan that is fully oven-safe, purely for its versatility.

BRAND

You want a cast-iron skillet that will work exceptionally well and last a long time, which often comes down to the quality of the brand you choose. There are a few top brands that have dominated the market for good reason.

Lodge is really the first name in the world of uncoated cast-iron cookware. The company has been around for more than 125 years, and their bare cast-iron products are dependably top quality. Their cookware is solidly built, and if taken care of properly, will last for generations. Although their pans aren't the cheapest you'll find on the market, they are extremely affordable. You'll pay less than $30 for the classic 12-inch skillet.

Lodge also offers enameled cast iron, but whereas their uncoated products are made in the United States, their enameled products are made in China, and the quality seems not quite as high or as consistent as that of the US-made products.

Le Creuset and Staub are the top name brands in the enameled cast-iron cookware world. Both are extremely high quality, and their price tags reflect that quality. If you want the best of the best, choose one of these brands. The 12-inch version of either brand will set you back around $200. If that is over your budget, Lodge enameled skillets are certainly decent and cost about half the price.

Lightweight cast-iron cookware is new to the scene, but there are a few brands that are making good names for themselves. Lodge has introduced their own line of lightweight cast-iron skillets, called Blacklock, and the quality is comparable to that of their classic cast-iron cookware. Butter Pat Industries and Field also make good-quality lightweight cast-iron skillets, both pricier than Lodge—Butter Pat's 12-inch skillet will run you close to $300 and Field's is around $200.

All About Cast Iron

A well-seasoned, properly cared-for cast-iron skillet can last for decades, far longer than any coated nonstick pan you'll find on the market. In fact, if properly maintained, the nonstick surface will actually improve with age. The key is in how you prepare and care for your pan over the years. Contrary to popular belief, caring for cast-iron cookware is not difficult, but it is crucial to its lifespan and utility. The process of seasoning and reseasoning your pan, cleaning, maintenance, and storage are all addressed here.

SEASONING

Seasoning your cast-iron skillet protects it and makes it nonstick. Seasoning simply means coating the pan with oil and then heating it so that the fat becomes bonded to the pan's surface. When the oiled pan is heated, the oil oxidizes, which creates a chemical reaction that bonds the fat with the metal, creating a durable, plastic-like, nonstick coating.

What Type of Oil to Use. You can use any neutral-flavor oil with a high smoke point. Corn, flaxseed, grapeseed, safflower, sunflower, and vegetable oils are all good choices.

When to Season. Season a new skillet by going through the oiling, heating, and cooling process at least two or three times before you use the pan for the first time. Even uncoated skillets sold as "preseasoned" require at least one more round of seasoning before use.

Each time you use your skillet, you can reseason it by heating it, wiping it with an oil-soaked paper towel, and then letting it cool to room temperature.

Occasionally, you'll need to go through the full seasoning process again. You'll know it's time when food begins sticking to your pan during cooking.

How to Season from Scratch. Follow these steps to season your new cast-iron skillet or to reseason one that needs a touch-up.

1. Start by scrubbing the pan. I like to scrub with a kosher salt or baking soda paste. Scrub off as much dust, residue, or rust as you can. Next, wash the pan well with hot water and, if you like, a mild dish soap. Dry it thoroughly.
2. Preheat the oven to 200°F. Place the skillet in the hot oven for 15 minutes. The heat will cause the metal to expand slightly, opening up its pores and giving the oil a way to seep in.
3. Spread a thin layer of oil on the skillet, coating the entire surface inside and out.
4. Raise the oven temperature to 400°F (you can use a higher heat, up to 500°F if your oven goes that high). Place the skillet upside down on the center rack, and place either a piece of aluminum foil or a baking sheet underneath to catch any dripping oil. Leave the skillet in the hot oven for 1 hour.
5. Turn off the oven's heat but leave the skillet inside for at least 2 hours to cool.
6. Repeat steps 2 through 5 at least two or three more times if you are seasoning a new skillet. If you are reseasoning a skillet, one time may be enough. In the end, you want the skillet to have a dark color and a glossy sheen.

CLEANING AND DRYING

Cleaning a cast-iron skillet isn't much different from cleaning any other skillet. Hot water and a good sponge are usually all you need. Add some dish soap if you need a bit more oomph. You can use a sponge, a natural-fiber scrubbing brush, or a plastic scrubber to help remove stuck-on food or rust. For really tough jobs, you can use a chainmail scrubber.

If you're having trouble removing stuck-on food, fill the skillet with hot water and bring it to a boil. Let the water boil in the skillet for a few minutes, which will be enough to break up most stuck-on food. If not, make a paste of coarse kosher salt or baking soda and warm water and use it to scour off the mess.

When you have finished cleaning your skillet, dry it well with a dish towel. Next, heat the pan briefly over medium heat and then rub a lightly oil-soaked paper towel over the interior. Wipe again with a clean paper towel to remove any excess oil. Allow the pan to cool and store it in a dry place.

Common Cast Iron Myths and Questions

There are lots of myths, misconceptions, and points of confusion around cooking in cast iron. So, let's clear up a few!

Q: I've heard cast-iron cookware is difficult to maintain. Is that true?

A: Not really. There are a few things you need to do to keep your cast-iron pans in top shape, but none of them is difficult or time-consuming. The first is to make sure that you properly season the pan before using (see the instructions on page 9) and reseason it as needed. Second, after using a cast-iron pan, be sure to wash it immediately, dry it well, heat it on the stove, and give it a swipe of oil. That's it!

Q: Can I use dish soap on my cast-iron cookware?

A: Yes! The most commonly held myth about cast-iron cookware is that dish soap will destroy the seasoning and/or surface of your skillet. It's easy to see where this myth comes from because the protective layer on a cast-iron skillet is created with a layer of oil, and dish soap is engineered to cut through oil. But dish soap will not strip the seasoning from your pan. The seasoning layer you create when you season a cast-iron pan is actually a layer of polymerized oil. This means that a chemical reaction has bonded the oil to the metal, creating a strong, plastic-like coating. A soap designed for hand washing dishes won't be able to strip that away. So, go ahead and soap up!

Q: Can I cook acidic foods like tomatoes in my cast-iron skillet?

A: Yes, with caveats. When acid comes into contact with the iron surface, it could cause iron to leach into your food. This can give food an unpleasant taste and can also be bad for your health. But in actuality, a good seasoning layer will prevent the acid from ever coming into contact with the metal. When your pan is newly seasoned, you might want to avoid cooking highly

continued >

acidic foods. But once you have a good seasoning layer, you don't need to worry about this.

Q: My cast-iron skillet is rusty. How do I fix it?

A: Don't fret! You can restore a rusty cast-iron skillet to its past glory. Use a plastic, natural, or steel-wool scrubber along with a paste of either coarse salt or baking soda and water to scour off the rust. Once all the rust is gone, wash the skillet well. Dry it thoroughly and then immediately season the pan following the instructions on page 9.

Q: Is older cast-iron cookware better than the new stuff?

A: Unfortunately, the answer seems to be yes. The modern process for finishing cast-iron cookware has been simplified for economy. Before World War II, cast-iron pans were polished to a smooth, satiny finish in the factory. After WW II, however, the process was streamlined, eliminating that step. When you buy a new cast-iron pan, you'll notice that the finish is a bit rough. But not to worry, a few extra rounds of seasoning can make it fully nonstick. Or shop for cast-iron cookware at thrift and antique stores.

Q: Can you use metal utensils with cast iron?

A: You can! Once seasoned, cast-iron cookware has a nonstick surface, but it's not a coating like Teflon. When you properly season cast iron, the oil actually bonds to the metal, creating a super strong surface. Even metal utensils won't be able to scratch through that coating.

STORING

Proper storage is important to keep your cast-iron skillet at peak performance level. Always be sure that the pan is clean and completely dry before putting it away. And be sure to choose a dry spot to store it—whether that is in a cabinet, on a shelf, or hanging on the wall. Moisture can cause your pan to rust, which can be remedied by scrubbing and reseasoning but is best prevented altogether.

If you store your cast-iron skillet stacked with other cast-iron skillets or any other type of skillet, it is a good idea to put a double layer of paper towels in the bottom. This will help keep the surface dry and also prevent any scratches or dings.

Your Speedy Cast-Iron Kitchen

This book is all about dishes that can be cooked in 30 minutes or less. They have short ingredient lists and quick cooking times. But if you really want to be able to cook meals in a flash, having a well-stocked kitchen is key.

PANTRY AND COUNTER

Here is a list of pantry and counter items you'll need to make this book's recipes. If your budget allows, choose organic/non-GMO products for your overall health, although it isn't necessary; these recipes will taste great regardless.

Beans. Canned beans are so easy to turn into a delicious and nutritious meal. I always have chickpeas, cannellini beans, pinto beans, and black beans in the pantry.

Black peppercorns and pepper grinder. Freshly ground black pepper adds a nice flavor punch to just about any savory dish.

Broth. Chicken or vegetable broth is the base of many sauces and soups.

Cooking oil. In addition to olive oil, I like safflower, sunflower, peanut, avocado, and coconut oils.

Flour and cornstarch. All-purpose flour is essential for baking, and cornstarch is used to thicken sauces.

Onions and garlic. These ingredients are the starting point of many a savory recipe.

Potatoes and sweet potatoes. These vegetables can be fried, sautéed, or roasted in your skillet and make great side dishes.

Salt. Kosher salt or sea salt is recommended for cooking. Choose salt that doesn't have anticaking ingredients or other additives.

Seasoning/spice mixes. With mixes, you get a whole lot of flavor with just one ingredient. At a bare minimum, I keep chili powder, curry powder, and Chinese five-spice powder on hand.

Spices. Keep your spice cabinet stocked with ground dried spices, and you'll always be able to whip up something tasty. My always-in-my-cupboard spices are cayenne, cinnamon, cloves, coriander, cumin, ginger, and paprika (sweet and smoked).

Tomatoes. Canned diced tomatoes can add bright flavor to all sorts of dishes.

REFRIGERATOR AND FREEZER

You'll find these items called for in the recipes in this book, so keep them on hand. Again, organic, non-GMO, and pasture-raised or grass-fed is best, but don't fret if your budget doesn't stretch to that.

Beef and pork. If you eat them, these proteins are always great starting points for a cast-iron skillet meal. Steak, chops, and other quick-cooking cuts can be quickly seared to caramelize the outside and seal in the flavor and juices. Many meats also benefit from being finished in a hot oven, which can also be done right in the skillet.

Butter. Butter is great to use for cast-iron cooking because it adds flavor while lubricating the pan surface. You can keep butter either in the refrigerator or in the freezer.

Chicken and fatty fish. Chicken cuts and salmon or cod are ideal for searing or roasting in cast iron.

Fresh vegetables. Vegetables such as broccoli, green beans, leafy greens, and squash make savory recipes nutritious and satisfying. They can be prepared as side dishes or cooked along with proteins and starches to make one-pan meals.

Frozen vegetables. Broccoli, corn, green beans, peas, and spinach can round out a quick meal when you don't have time to go to the store for fresh produce.

Cast-Iron Sidekicks

Once you have a good cast-iron skillet, you are ready to start cooking. These items are some that you may find useful to have on hand to support your cast-iron skillet cooking. You may already own many of them, such as wooden spoons or tongs.

Chainmail scrubber. A scrubber made of metal chainmail can be used for tough skillet-cleaning jobs.

Metal spatula. Remember that your cast-iron skillet is tough, so you don't need to worry about scratching the surface with metal utensils. A sturdy, thin metal spatula with a straight edge is ideal for lifting food from the skillet.

Natural-bristle scrubber. A good stiff, natural-bristle brush will help you clean your skillet without running the risk of damaging the surface.

Silicone handle protectors. These protectors slip over the handle of your cast-iron skillet to make it safe to touch when hot.

Silicone oven mitts. These mitts are simply the best for protecting your hands from the high heat of cast-iron cookware.

Silicone trivet. Set your hot skillet on this trivet to protect your table and countertop.

Skillet lid. Most cast-iron skillets don't come with a lid, but you can buy one separately. Get a lid that is the same diameter as your skillet and has a looped handle in the center that is also made of cast iron, ensuring that it is just as oven-safe as the skillet. (Tip: If you don't have a lid, use a baking sheet to cover your skillet!)

Tongs. These tools are handy for turning foods such as chicken breasts or sausages. You can use metal tongs or metal tongs with silicone or nylon tips. Avoid plastic tongs, which may melt on contact with hot cast iron.

Wooden spoons/spatulas. These tools are great for stirring sauces and are preferable to plastic ones that may melt. You can use just about any wooden utensils in your skillet.

Quick Cast-Iron Cooking Tips

Cooking in cast iron is a bit different from cooking in other types of cookware. Here are my five favorite quick tips for cooking cast-iron meals.

Always use plenty of fat. Fat adds flavor to your food, prevents it from sticking, and helps maintain the lovely seasoning on the pan that you worked so hard to create. Every time you cook a dish with a good amount of fat in it, you add to that seasoning layer, so bring on the bacon!

Preheat the oven. Always read the recipe all the way through before starting to prep or cook. That way you'll know if, for instance, you need to preheat the oven for finishing the dish.

Preheat the skillet over low heat for about 5 minutes before cooking. This step will ensure that the pan is fully heated throughout.

Get the pan very hot before adding proteins. Proteins like steak, chicken, and fish will stick if you put them in the pan before it is thoroughly heated. For searing meat and fish, you want the pan to be very, very hot before adding them.

Use heavy-duty oven mitts. One of the great things about cooking in cast iron is that it gets extremely hot. That's wonderful news for cooking but can be dangerous. Be sure to protect your hands well with sturdy oven mitts. I prefer silicone oven mitts because they do the best job of protecting hands. You can also get a silicone handle protector that slides over the skillet handle.

About the Recipes

The cast-iron skillet's versatility makes it perfect for cooking all sorts of recipes. Because you can use the skillet both on the stovetop and in the oven, the possibilities for meal preparation are endless.

I've selected dishes for this book that are especially well suited to cast-iron cooking and that are also quick and easy to prepare. These recipes include some of my favorite skillet dishes, updated classics, adaptations of dishes from around the world, and recipes that use the skillet in unexpected ways.

This book focuses on cast-iron skillet recipes that can be made in 30 minutes or less. Each uses a seasoned 12-inch cast-iron skillet as the primary cooking vessel, but a 10- or 14-inch skillet will also work for most of the recipes.. There are dishes for breakfast and brunch, main dishes, sides, snacks, and sweets. With these delicious, quick-to-make recipes, you'll soon be using your cast-iron skillet more than you ever dreamed possible.

RECIPE LABELS

To make it easy to choose recipes based on dietary restrictions, I've labeled recipes that conform to certain food restrictions: dairy-free, gluten-free, vegan, or vegetarian.

RECIPE TIPS

Many recipes also include useful tips in the following categories:

Cast-iron tip: These tips provide help or further clarification around using the cast-iron skillet or a heads-up regarding cleanup.

Make it easier: These tips give advice and suggestions to make prep and/or cooking even easier, such as using a store-bought seasoning mix or prepping part or all of the recipe in advance.

Variation tip: These tips offer suggestions for swapping ingredients to vary the flavors or to make the recipe conform to a specific dietary restriction.

CHAPTER 2

BREAKFAST AND BRUNCH

Shakshuka, page 28

Maple, Almond, and Blueberry Oatmeal Bake

Serves 4 / **Prep time: 5 minutes** / **Cook time: 25 minutes**

This hearty breakfast is a great example of the versatility of the cast-iron skillet. First, you use the skillet to toast the oats and almonds on the stove-top. Next, you add fruit, milk, and an egg. Then, the whole thing goes in the oven to cook through. On a cold winter morning, this breakfast bake is just the thing.

2 tablespoons unsalted butter

½ cup slivered almonds

2 cups gluten-free old-fashioned rolled oats

1 teaspoon baking powder

1 teaspoon ground cinnamon

½ teaspoon kosher salt

2 cups fresh or frozen blueberries, divided

1¾ cups milk

1 large egg

¼ cup maple syrup, plus more for drizzling

1. Preheat the oven to 375°F.

2. Heat a skillet over medium heat. Put the butter in the skillet and let it melt, swirling it around to coat the pan. Add the almonds and oats and cook, stirring constantly, for about 2 minutes, or until they give off a toasty aroma. Add the baking powder, cinnamon, and salt and stir to mix, then spread the oatmeal into an even layer in the skillet. Scatter 1½ cups of blueberries over the oatmeal.

3. In a bowl, whisk together the milk, egg, and maple syrup. Pour this mixture into the skillet over the oatmeal and berries. Scatter the remaining ½ cup of berries over the top.

4. Bake for 25 minutes or until set.

5. Serve warm, drizzled with more maple syrup.

Variation tip: In the fall or winter months, diced apples or pears work well in this dish. In the summer, substitute peaches or nectarines, and in the spring, use strawberries.

Strawberry Clafoutis

Serves 4 / **Prep time: 5 minutes** / Cook time: **25 minutes**

Clafoutis is sort of a cross between a custard and a baked, fruit-filled pancake. It is easy to make and a great way to highlight fresh, seasonal fruit. To make clafoutis, fresh fruit is layered into the skillet, and a pancake-like batter is poured over the top. Then, it is baked until set.

2 cups fresh or frozen strawberries, halved or quartered

2 large eggs

½ cup milk

½ cup all-purpose flour

¼ cup sugar

¼ teaspoon kosher salt

1. Preheat the oven to 375°F.

2. Arrange the berries in the bottom of a skillet in a single layer.

3. In a bowl, whisk together the eggs, milk, flour, sugar, and salt. Pour the mixture over the berries in the skillet.

4. Bake for about 25 minutes, or until the top is golden and the center is set.

Variation tip: You can make this with just about any fruit you have on hand. Cherries are traditional (the French leave the pits in, but I advise using pitted cherries!). Other great options are blueberries, nectarines, or peaches.

Ricotta and Lemon Dutch Baby

Serves **6** / Prep time: **5 minutes** / Cook time: **22 minutes**

A Dutch baby is a puffed-up pancake that is baked in the oven, similar to clafoutis but puffier and less custardy. A cast-iron skillet is the perfect cooking vessel because it gets very hot and can be placed in a very hot oven, which is crucial for getting the pancake to puff up.

3 large eggs

¾ cup ricotta cheese, divided

⅔ cup whole milk

⅔ cup all-purpose flour

3 teaspoons grated lemon zest, divided

½ teaspoon vanilla extract

⅛ teaspoon kosher salt

2 tablespoons unsalted butter, cut into pieces

1 tablespoon confectioners' sugar

2 teaspoons freshly squeezed lemon juice

1. Place a skillet in the oven, and preheat the oven to 450°F.

2. In a medium bowl, using an electric mixer, or in a stand mixer, beat the eggs at high speed until they become frothy and pale yellow. Add ¼ cup of ricotta, the milk, flour, 2 teaspoons of lemon zest, vanilla, and salt and beat until smooth.

3. Remove the skillet from the oven, and melt the butter in it, swirling to coat the bottom of the pan. Pour the batter into the skillet and return it to the hot oven.

4. Bake for 18 to 22 minutes, or until the Dutch baby puffs up and turns golden brown.

5. While the Dutch baby is in the oven, combine the remaining ½ cup of ricotta with the remaining 1 teaspoon of lemon zest, the confectioners' sugar, and the lemon juice and whisk to combine.

6. To serve, dollop the ricotta mixture on top.

Variation tip: Make a quick blueberry sauce to drizzle over the top by combining ⅓ cup of sugar, 1 tablespoon of cornstarch, ¼ cup of water, and 1½ cups of fresh or frozen blueberries and microwaving the mixture on high in 1-minute intervals, until the mixture is bubbling and thick.

Chocolate Chip Pancakes

Serves **4** / Prep time: **5 minutes** / Cook time: **10 minutes**

I have the best memories of the rare occasions during my childhood when I was allowed to have chocolate chip pancakes for breakfast. Is there anything better? I like to top these with whipped cream and fresh berries, but you could also just add a dusting of confectioners' sugar or eat them plain.

1½ cups all-purpose flour

2 tablespoons sugar

1 tablespoon baking powder

1 teaspoon kosher salt

1½ cups milk

1 large egg

3 tablespoons unsalted butter, melted

¾ cup mini chocolate chips

1 tablespoon cooking oil, plus more as needed

1. In a large bowl, whisk together the flour, sugar, baking powder, and salt.

2. Add the milk, egg, and butter and whisk until well combined. Stir in the chocolate chips.

3. Heat a skillet over medium-high heat. Add the oil to the pan and let it heat for 30 seconds to 1 minute.

4. Use a ladle to pour about ¼ cup of batter at a time into the skillet. Cook for about 2 minutes, or until the bottom of the pancake is golden brown and you see bubbles pop on the top and not immediately fill in with wet batter. Reduce the heat to medium if needed to keep the underside from burning. Flip the pancake and cook for about 2 more minutes, or until the second side is golden brown.

5. Repeat with the remaining batter, cooking three or four pancakes at a time as your skillet allows. Add more oil if needed.

6. Serve hot.

Variation tip: For double chocolate pancakes, add 2 tablespoons of unsweetened cocoa powder to the batter along with the other dry ingredients in step 1.

Glazed Cinnamon Skillet Cake

Serves 6 / **Prep time: 5 minutes** / **Cook time: 25 minutes**

This quick skillet cake has all the flavor of yeasted cinnamon rolls but can be made in a fraction of the time. The cake cooks quickly in a 12-inch skillet. If you only have a 10-inch skillet, you can use that, but you may have to bake the cake a bit longer to cook it through.

FOR THE CAKE

8 tablespoons (1 stick) unsalted butter, at room temperature, plus more for greasing the skillet

1 cup light brown sugar

2 large eggs

2 cups all-purpose flour

1½ teaspoons baking powder

1½ teaspoons ground cinnamon

1 teaspoon kosher salt

¾ cup milk

FOR THE GLAZE

2 tablespoons confectioners' sugar, plus more as needed

2 tablespoons milk, plus more as needed

TO MAKE THE CAKE

1. Preheat the oven to 375°F and coat the inside of a 12-inch skillet with butter.

2. In a large bowl, cream together the butter and brown sugar with a wooden spoon until the mixture is creamy and well combined. Add the eggs one at a time, beating after each addition until fully incorporated.

3. In a separate bowl, stir together the flour, baking powder, cinnamon, and salt.

4. Add half of the flour mixture to the butter-and-sugar mixture and beat to incorporate. Add the milk and beat to incorporate, then add the remaining flour mixture and beat to incorporate.

5. Transfer the batter to the skillet, smoothing the top and pushing it into the pan with a silicone spatula.

6. Bake for 25 minutes, or until a toothpick inserted into the center comes out clean.

7. While the cake is baking, in a small bowl, stir together the confectioners' sugar and milk until smooth. If it is too thick, you can add a touch more milk. If it is too thin, add a bit more confectioners' sugar.

8. Remove the cake from the oven and let it cool for a few minutes before drizzling the glaze over the top. Serve warm or at room temperature.

Variation tip: If you want to give this cake an extra dose of cinnamon, combine 2 tablespoons of granulated sugar and 1 teaspoon of ground cinnamon and sprinkle it over the top of the batter before baking.

Peach and Brown Sugar Coffee Cake

Serves **8** / Prep time: **5 minutes** / Cook time: **25 minutes**

I know what you're thinking: Cake for breakfast? But this one has a luscious layer of fresh peaches and goes so well with a cup of hot coffee. See, it's *coffee* cake. That automatically qualifies it as a breakfast food, right? A 12-inch skillet is best for this cake, but you can use a 10-inch skillet and bake the cake a few minutes longer.

12 tablespoons (1½ sticks) unsalted butter, divided

½ cup packed light brown sugar

2 medium peaches, cut into thin wedges

1 cup granulated sugar

2 large eggs

2 cups all-purpose flour

2 teaspoons baking powder

¾ teaspoon ground cinnamon

¾ teaspoon kosher salt

⅔ cup sour cream

2 teaspoons vanilla extract

1. Preheat the oven to 375°F.

2. In a skillet over low heat, melt 4 tablespoons of butter, swirling it around to coat the pan. Remove the pan from the heat and sprinkle the brown sugar in an even layer in the skillet.

3. Arrange the peach slices in a single layer on top of the brown sugar.

4. In a large bowl, cream together the remaining 8 tablespoons of butter and the granulated sugar with a wooden spoon until creamy and well combined. Add the eggs, one at a time, beating after each addition until fully incorporated.

5. In a medium bowl, whisk together the flour, baking powder, cinnamon, and salt.

6. Add the flour mixture to the butter mixture and beat to incorporate. Add the sour cream and vanilla and mix until well incorporated.

7. Pour the batter over the peaches. Spread the batter into an even layer in the skillet with the back of a wooden spoon or an offset spatula.

8. Bake for 20 to 25 minutes, or until the cake is golden brown on top.

9. Remove the skillet from the oven, and let the cake cool in the pan for a few minutes.

10. To serve, run a knife around the sides of the cake to release it from the skillet. Carefully invert the cake onto a serving platter. Serve warm or at room temperature.

Variation tip: You can make this coffee cake with just about any soft fruit. Pineapple is classic, of course, or you can use nectarines, berries, or pears.

Shakshuka

Serves 4 / **Prep time: 5 minutes** / **Cook time: 25 minutes**

Shakshuka is a simple dish of eggs poached in a spicy tomato sauce. This meal is popular throughout North Africa and the Middle East, where it is often served with crusty bread for scooping. If you like a bit of spice, dollop some harissa on top. Serve this dish with lots of crusty bread for sopping up the sauce.

2 tablespoons extra-virgin olive oil

1 onion, diced

3 garlic cloves, crushed and thinly sliced

1 tablespoon paprika

2 teaspoons ground cumin

1 (15-ounce) can diced tomatoes with their juices

1 red bell pepper, seeded and diced

1 jalapeño pepper, seeded and diced

1 tablespoon tomato paste

1 dried bay leaf

1 teaspoon kosher salt

4 large eggs

1. Preheat the oven to 400°F.

2. In a skillet over medium-high heat, heat the oil. Add the onion and garlic, and cook, stirring, for about 5 minutes, or until softened. Stir in the paprika and cumin. Add the tomatoes with their juices, bell pepper, jalapeño, tomato paste, bay leaf, and salt. Bring the mixture to a boil and cook, stirring occasionally, for about 5 minutes, or until it thickens.

3. Make 4 wells in the sauce with the back of a spoon and crack 1 egg into each. Transfer the skillet to the oven. Bake for about 12 minutes, or until the egg whites are set and the yolks are still a bit runny.

4. Before serving, remove and discard the bay leaf. Spoon the saucy vegetable mixture onto serving plates, along with 1 egg per person, and serve immediately.

Savory Dutch Baby with Spinach and Cheese

Serves 4 / **Prep time: 10 minutes** / **Cook time: 20 minutes**

This puffed-up, oven-baked pancake is more commonly made with fruit, but this version with cheese and greens is a great savory alternative. Because it gets so hot and can go in the oven, the cast-iron skillet is the traditional cooking vessel for a Dutch baby.

4 tablespoons (½ stick) unsalted butter, divided

4 large eggs, at room temperature

⅔ cup whole milk, at room temperature

⅔ cup all-purpose flour

¼ cup freshly grated Parmesan cheese

¾ teaspoon kosher salt, plus a pinch

2 cups baby spinach or arugula

8 ounces fresh mozzarella cheese, cubed

¼ cup julienned fresh basil leaves

1. Preheat the oven to 450°F.

2. Put 2 tablespoons of butter in a skillet and heat the skillet in the oven for about 5 minutes.

3. In the microwave or a small saucepan, melt the remaining 2 tablespoons of butter. Whisk the melted butter together with the eggs, milk, flour, Parmesan, and ¾ teaspoon of salt until completely smooth.

4. Remove the skillet from the oven and immediately pour the batter into the pan, tilting it if necessary to ensure that the batter is evenly distributed. Bake for 15 to 20 minutes until the Dutch baby is puffed and golden brown on top.

5. Remove the pancake from the oven and immediately layer the baby spinach and mozzarella on top. Sprinkle with the remaining pinch of salt, garnish with the basil, and serve immediately.

Variation tip: Substitute chard for the baby spinach by precooking it while the pancake is in the oven. In a skillet over medium-high heat, heat 1 tablespoon of butter. Add 8 to 10 julienned chard leaves to the skillet with a pinch of salt. Cook, stirring occasionally, for 5 minutes, or until wilted.

Pesto Breakfast Pizza

Serves **2** / Prep time: **12 minutes** / Cook time: **10 minutes**

I love cold pizza for breakfast, but this is even better: a nice, thin, golden-brown crust topped with pesto, cheese, and eggs that are baked right on top. This recipe uses half a standard pizza dough recipe, so you can make two, or make it two days in a row! If you want a meaty version, add cooked bacon or sausage before baking, or top with a few slices of prosciutto once the pizza is out of the oven. This recipe works best with a 12-inch skillet. If you have a smaller skillet, use a bit less dough if you want to maintain the thin crust, or use the same amount for a slightly thicker crust.

8 ounces pizza dough, enough for 1 (12-inch) pizza

¾ cup pesto

½ cup shredded mozzarella cheese

4 large eggs

Salt

Freshly ground black pepper

2 scallions, thinly sliced

Freshly grated Parmesan cheese, for garnish

1. Preheat the oven to 425°F.

2. Roll or stretch the dough into about a 12-inch circle. Press the dough into a skillet (it's okay if it goes up the sides a bit).

3. Spread the pesto over the dough in an even layer. Sprinkle the mozzarella in an even layer over the pesto. Make 4 wells in the cheese, evenly spaced around the pizza, and crack 1 egg into each. Sprinkle salt and pepper over the eggs.

4. Bake for 10 to 12 minutes, or until the crust is golden brown and the egg whites are set.

5. Remove the pizza from the skillet and sprinkle the scallions and Parmesan over the top.

6. Cut into 4 wedges, with 1 egg in the center of each, and serve immediately.

Make it easier: These days you can buy great pizza dough in the refrigerator section of many supermarkets, so don't feel like you have to make your own.

Goat Cheese, Spinach, and Mushroom Frittata

Serves 6 / Prep time: 5 minutes / Cook time: 15 minutes

I love serving frittata for everything from a make-ahead weekday breakfast to a festive lunch or brunch. Frittatas only take a handful of ingredients, and they're super versatile. Try adding other vegetables you have on hand.

3 tablespoons extra-virgin olive oil, divided

2 garlic cloves, minced

8 ounces cremini or button mushrooms, sliced

½ teaspoon kosher salt, plus a pinch

8 large eggs

5 ounces (½ [10-ounce] package) frozen spinach, thawed and excess water squeezed out

4 ounces crumbled goat cheese

2 scallions, thinly sliced

½ teaspoon freshly ground black pepper

1. In a skillet over medium heat, heat 1 tablespoon of oil. Add the garlic, mushrooms, and a pinch of salt and cook, stirring frequently, for about 5 minutes, or until the vegetables soften and begin to brown. Remove from the heat.

2. In a large bowl, whisk the eggs. Add the remaining ½ teaspoon of salt, spinach, cheese, scallions, pepper, and the mushrooms and stir to mix.

3. Preheat the broiler.

4. Wipe out the skillet with a paper towel and add the remaining 2 tablespoons of oil. Heat the skillet over medium-high heat. Pour in the egg mixture and cook for about 4 minutes, or just until the eggs are set on the bottom.

5. Transfer the skillet to the broiler and cook for about 3 minutes, or until the eggs are set in the center and the top is golden brown.

6. Run a knife around the sides of the frittata to release it from the skillet, then carefully invert it onto a serving platter. Cut into wedges and serve.

Cast-iron tip: To keep your eggs from sticking to the skillet, make sure that the pan is very hot before you add them.

Bacon and Egg Skillet Breakfast

Serves 4 / **Prep time: 5 minutes** / **Cook time: 20 minutes**

I'm a savory breakfast lover, so I'm all over any breakfast that includes bacon, eggs, potatoes, and cheese all cooked in a single pan. It is simply everything you want in a savory breakfast—crunchy, creamy, salty, and incredibly satisfying.

4 thick-cut bacon slices, diced

1 pound Idaho or russet potatoes, peeled and diced small

1 small onion, diced

½ teaspoon kosher salt

¼ teaspoon freshly ground black pepper

4 large eggs, lightly beaten

1 cup shredded Cheddar cheese

1. Heat a skillet over medium-high heat. Add the bacon and cook, turning once, for about 5 minutes, or until browned and crisp. Remove the bacon from the skillet and drain on a paper towel-lined plate. Drain the excess fat from the skillet.

2. Add the potatoes, onion, salt, and pepper to the skillet and cook, stirring occasionally, for 8 to 10 minutes, or until softened.

3. Add the eggs to the skillet and cook, stirring frequently, until the eggs are about half set. Add the cheese and continue to cook, stirring, until the eggs are set and the cheese is melted.

4. Serve the eggs with the bacon on the side.

Cast-iron tip: Cooking bacon, or any fatty food, in cast iron is great for helping build up the seasoning. So, obviously: Eat more bacon!

Sausage and Sweet Potato Hash

Serves 4 / **Prep time: 5 minutes** / **Cook time: 25 minutes**

This satisfying dish is perfect for breakfast, brunch, or lunch. Of course, it also works for "breakfast for dinner." You can use any type of sausage you like here—pork, chicken, maple, spicy, or even vegetarian.

1 pound loose gluten-free breakfast sausage

2 tablespoons olive oil

1 onion, thinly sliced

2 garlic cloves, minced

2 sweet potatoes, peeled and diced small

1 teaspoon kosher salt, plus more for sprinkling

¼ teaspoon freshly ground black pepper, plus more for sprinkling

¼ teaspoon ground paprika

4 large eggs

4 tablespoons shredded cheese of choice, divided

2 tablespoons chopped fresh flat-leaf parsley

1. Preheat the oven to 400°F.

2. Heat a skillet over medium-high heat. Cook the sausage, stirring occasionally, for about 5 minutes, or until cooked through. Remove the sausage from the skillet.

3. Add the oil to the skillet, then the onion, and cook, stirring frequently, for about 3 minutes, or until the onion begins to soften. Add the garlic, sweet potatoes, salt, pepper, and paprika and stir to mix well. Cook, stirring frequently, for 10 more minutes, or until the sweet potatoes begin to brown. Stir in the cooked sausage and cook for about 2 more minutes, or until heated through.

4. Make 4 indentations in the hash and crack 1 egg into each. Sprinkle some salt, pepper, and 1 tablespoon of shredded cheese over each egg.

5. Transfer the skillet to the oven and bake for about 5 minutes, or until the eggs are just set.

6. Serve each person 1 egg on a "nest" of hash. Garnish with the parsley just before serving.

Variation tip: If you don't like sweet potatoes, you can use regular potatoes, like Idaho or russet.

CHAPTER 3

SIDES

Oven-Roasted Asparagus with Lemon, page 36

Oven-Roasted Asparagus with Lemon

Serves 4 / **Prep time: 5 minutes** / **Cook time: 25 minutes**

When fresh asparagus is in season, it is one of my favorite vegetables to roast in the oven. It's quick and easy—just toss the asparagus with olive oil, salt, and pepper and roast for 20 to 25 minutes (depending on how thick the spears are). The bright acidity of lemon pairs really well with the woody flavor of asparagus. Just a squeeze of fresh lemon juice and a sprinkle of the zest make all the difference.

1½ pounds asparagus, trimmed

3 tablespoons olive oil

¾ teaspoon kosher salt

½ teaspoon freshly ground black pepper

Juice of 1 lemon

Grated zest of 1 lemon

1. Preheat the oven to 400°F.

2. In a skillet, toss the asparagus with the oil and then spread it into a single layer (or as close to a single layer as possible). Sprinkle with the salt and pepper.

3. Roast for 20 to 25 minutes, or until crisp-tender. The cooking time will depend on how thick or thin the asparagus spears are.

4. Remove the skillet from the oven and drizzle the lemon juice over the top.

5. Garnish with the lemon zest and serve immediately.

Variation tip: Just before serving, grate Parmesan cheese over the top. Lemon and Parmesan make a classic flavor combination that will elevate this simple vegetable side to a whole new level.

Skillet-Roasted Potatoes with Fresh Herbs

Serves 4 / Prep time: 5 minutes / Cook time: 20 minutes

Roasted potatoes are a great all-purpose side dish. These potatoes pair perfectly with a meat, chicken, fish, or vegetarian meal, and they're easy to make, too. Adding chopped fresh herbs kicks the delicious factor up a notch with very little added effort. The key here is to cut the potatoes into thin slices so that they cook quickly.

2 tablespoons olive oil

2 tablespoons chopped fresh flat-leaf parsley, plus more for garnish

1 tablespoon chopped fresh thyme

2 garlic cloves, roughly chopped

¾ teaspoon kosher salt

½ teaspoon freshly ground black pepper

1½ pounds fingerling, Yukon Gold, or other small, thin-skinned potatoes, cut into ⅛-inch-thick slices

1. Preheat the oven to 400°F.

2. In a small bowl, stir together the oil, parsley, thyme, garlic, salt, and pepper.

3. In a skillet, toss the potatoes with the oil mixture to coat the potatoes well.

4. Spread the potatoes into a single layer (or as close to a single layer as possible) in the skillet.

5. Roast, stirring once or twice, for about 20 minutes, or until the potatoes are cooked through and browned on the outside. Serve hot, garnished with extra parsley.

Make it easier: If you don't mind waiting a little longer, you can just halve or quarter the potatoes. They'll take 10 to 15 minutes longer to cook.

Corn Fritters

Serves **4** / Prep time: **5 minutes** / Cook time: **20 minutes**

These crispy fritters make a great quick and savory side or snack. You can add some punch by adding a diced jalapeño pepper or two to the batter. Or try adding bacon, sausage, or shredded cheese. I've been known to serve these as savory pancakes for brunch, too.

1 cup finely ground cornmeal

½ cup all-purpose flour

1 teaspoon kosher salt

1 teaspoon ground cumin

2 large eggs

1½ cups plain whole-milk yogurt

Kernels from 2 ears of corn (or about 2 cups frozen corn)

Cooking oil, for frying

1. In a medium bowl, whisk together the cornmeal, flour, salt, and cumin. Add the eggs and whisk to combine well. Stir in the yogurt and corn.

2. Fill a skillet with about 1 inch of oil and heat it over medium-high heat until the oil shimmers. Ladle about ¼ cup of batter into the pan for each fritter. Cook for about 3 minutes, or until the fritters are golden brown on the bottom. Flip and cook for about 3 more minutes, or until crisp and browned. Drain on paper towels. Repeat with the remaining batter. Serve hot.

Make it easier: If you want to avoid splatters and use less oil, you can make these fritters into flatter corn cakes and pan-fry them.

Roasted Winter Squash with Parmesan and Sage

Serves 4 / **Prep time:** **10 minutes** / **Cook time:** **20 minutes**

Butternut squash, like pumpkin, is a quintessential fall or winter vegetable. In this version, butternut squash is flavored with Parmesan cheese, garlic, and fresh sage. The sweet squash becomes wonderfully caramelized as it roasts in the skillet, making it the perfect side for your holiday table.

1 (2- to 3-pound) butternut squash, peeled and diced

2 tablespoons extra-virgin olive oil

4 garlic cloves, minced

1 teaspoon kosher salt

½ teaspoon freshly ground black pepper

1 cup freshly grated Parmesan cheese, divided

1 tablespoon chopped fresh sage

1. Preheat the oven to 400°F.

2. In a large bowl, toss together the squash, oil, garlic, salt, pepper, and ½ cup of cheese. Transfer the mixture to a skillet and spread it into a single layer.

3. Roast for 10 minutes, stir the squash, and spread it out again into a single layer. Sprinkle the remaining ½ cup of cheese on top and return the skillet to the oven.

4. Roast for about 10 more minutes, or until the top is golden brown and the squash is tender.

5. Just before serving, sprinkle the fresh sage over the top.

Variation tip: You can use any type of winter squash for this dish. Pumpkin and delicata squash are both great substitutes for butternut.

Bacon Braised Greens

Serves 4 / **Prep time: 5 minutes** / **Cook time: 25 minutes**

Collard greens on their own can be a bit dull, but pair them with meaty bacon and braise them in broth, and they are completely transformed. The hearty greens take on the flavors of the bacon and shallot and become perfectly tender. Serve these greens alongside roasted chicken or chicken potpie.

4 ounces bacon, diced

1 small shallot, diced

1½ pounds collard greens, stemmed and julienned

1½ cups chicken broth

¾ teaspoon kosher salt

½ teaspoon freshly ground black pepper

1. In a skillet over medium-high heat, cook the bacon for about 3 minutes, or until the fat begins to render. Add the shallot and cook, stirring occasionally, for about 4 more minutes, or until the shallot is softened and the bacon is browned.

2. Add the greens and toss to mix them with the bacon and shallot and coat them with the fat. Stir in the broth, salt, and pepper. Cover with a lid or aluminum foil and reduce the heat to medium. Cook for about 15 minutes, or until the greens are very tender. Serve hot.

Variation tip: You can substitute any sturdy greens for the collards here. I like to cook chard, kale, or mustard greens this way, too.

Blistered Green Beans with Shallots

Serves **4** / Prep time: **5 minutes** / Cook time: **15 minutes**

You'll never think of green beans as a boring side again. This cooking method makes them perfectly craveable, and the recipe uses only a handful of basic pantry ingredients. For an Asian twist, you might use a mix of cooking oil and sesame oil and season the beans with a dash of soy sauce after cooking.

3 tablespoons extra-virgin olive oil

1 small shallot, diced

1 pound green beans, dried well

½ teaspoon kosher salt

¼ teaspoon freshly ground black pepper

1. In a skillet over high heat, heat the oil until it shimmers. Add the shallot and cook, stirring occasionally, for about 3 minutes, or until softened.

2. Add the beans and cook without stirring for about 3 minutes. Continue to cook, tossing the beans occasionally, for about 5 more minutes, or until they are tender and charred and blistered in places.

3. Add the salt and pepper and toss to distribute. Serve hot.

Cast-iron tip: For this recipe, you want the beans to become blistered and blackened. To do that, you need to make sure that the pan is very hot before you add the beans.

Cheesy Jalapeño Corn Bread

Serves 8 / Prep time: **5 minutes** / Cook time: **25 minutes**

Cooking corn bread in a hot cast-iron skillet creates a crispy outer edge that's so irresistible, you'll never want to cook it in a regular cake pan again. I love the spicy kick of jalapeño peppers, but you can leave them out if you prefer a milder version, or substitute mild green chiles.

2½ tablespoons melted unsalted butter, plus more for greasing the skillet

1¼ cups stone-ground cornmeal

1 cup fresh corn kernels (from about 2 ears), or frozen

¾ teaspoon kosher salt

½ teaspoon baking soda

1 cup buttermilk

1 cup (about 4 ounces) shredded sharp Cheddar cheese

1 or 2 jalapeño peppers, seeded and minced

2 scallions, thinly sliced

1½ tablespoons honey

2 large eggs, lightly beaten

1. Preheat the oven to 400°F. Brush a 12-inch skillet with melted butter.

2. In a large bowl, whisk together the cornmeal, corn, salt, and baking soda.

3. In a small bowl, stir together the buttermilk, cheese, jalapeños, scallions, melted butter, honey, and eggs. Whisk the wet ingredients into the dry ingredients until just combined.

4. Spoon the batter into the prepared skillet and bake for about 25 minutes, or until a tester inserted into the center comes out clean.

5. Remove the skillet from the oven and set on a wire rack to cool a bit before serving.

6. Cut into wedges and serve warm or at room temperature.

Variation tip: Make this bread even more irresistible by adding bacon. Cook 4 slices of bacon in the skillet. Chop the bacon and add it to the batter, and use the bacon fat to grease the skillet.

Garlic Herb Biscuits

Makes 12 biscuits / Prep time: **10 minutes** / Cook time: **20 minutes**

Who can resist flaky, buttery biscuits studded with garlic and fresh herbs? Serve these biscuits with roasted or grilled meats, or as a savory breakfast. Whether smothered with gravy or spread with butter, they make any meal seem extra special.

8 tablespoons (1 stick) cold unsalted butter, plus 2 tablespoons melted

3 cups all-purpose flour

2 teaspoons baking powder

1 teaspoon kosher salt

2 tablespoons chopped fresh basil, parsley, oregano, or thyme (or a combination)

2 tablespoons minced fresh chives (or thinly sliced scallions)

1 garlic clove, finely minced

1¾ cups buttermilk

1. Preheat the oven to 400°F.

2. Swirl 2 tablespoons of melted butter around a skillet (you can melt the butter in the skillet by leaving it in the oven for a few minutes), coating the entire bottom and the sides of the pan.

3. In a large bowl, whisk together the flour, baking powder, and salt. Using the large holes of a box grater, grate the remaining 8 tablespoons of cold butter into the flour. Use a fork to mix the butter into the flour until it resembles a coarse meal. Add the chopped basil, chives, and garlic and mix to combine. Stir in the buttermilk until the dough comes together.

4. Use a large cookie scoop or a ¼-cup dry measuring cup to scoop the dough into the skillet, leaving as much space between the biscuits as possible (the skillet will be crowded).

5. Bake for about 20 minutes, or until golden brown.

6. Remove from the oven and serve warm.

Make it easier: Chill the butter in the freezer for 30 minutes before starting this recipe to make it easy to grate into the flour and create even flakier biscuits.

CHAPTER 4

PLANT-BASED MEALS

Goat Cheese and Pesto Pizza, page 51

Grilled Brie and Pear Sandwiches with Honey and Thyme

Serves 2 / Prep time: **10 minutes** / Cook time: **10 minutes**

This sandwich perfectly blends sweet and savory flavors. Gooey Brie cheese is balanced with sweet honey and fresh thyme leaves. Tender greens like arugula or baby spinach add color and textural contrast. This recipe serves two, but you can easily double the batch.

4 tablespoons (½ stick) unsalted butter, at room temperature

4 slices rustic French or Italian bread

6 to 8 slices Brie cheese

1½ teaspoons chopped fresh thyme leaves

Freshly ground black pepper

2 teaspoons honey

1 firm but ripe pear, such as Bosc or Bartlett, sliced

1 cup arugula or baby spinach leaves

1. Butter one side of each of the bread slices.

2. Heat a skillet over medium heat. Place 2 bread slices into the hot skillet, buttered-side down. Arrange the Brie on top of each slice of bread. Sprinkle the thyme and pepper over the cheese, then drizzle the honey on top. Add the pear slices and then the arugula.

3. Top with the remaining 2 slices of bread, buttered-side up.

4. Cook for about 4 minutes, or until the bottom is golden brown.

5. Carefully flip each sandwich to the other side and cook until the sandwich is golden brown on the bottom and the cheese is melted.

6. Remove from the skillet, cut each sandwich in half, and serve immediately.

Variation tip: Feel free to switch up the cheese in this sandwich. Other great choices are fontina, Taleggio, and Gruyère, which are all great melting cheeses.

Black Bean, Mushroom, and Spinach Burritos

Serves 6 / Prep time: **5 minutes** / Cook time: **15 minutes**

These vegetarian burritos are loaded with mushrooms, spinach, and black beans. You can serve them with extra salsa and shredded cheese and top them with guacamole or sour cream if you're feeling fancy.

6 burrito-size flour tortillas

1 tablespoon olive oil

1 onion, diced

2 garlic cloves, minced

12 ounces button or cremini mushrooms, sliced

1 tablespoon chili powder

1 teaspoon ground cumin

Kosher salt

4 ounces spinach leaves, chopped

1 (15-ounce) can black beans, drained and rinsed

1½ cups shredded Cheddar cheese

½ cup salsa

1. Preheat the oven to 350°F.

2. Wrap the tortillas in aluminum foil and put them in the oven to heat for about 10 minutes.

3. While the tortillas are heating, in a skillet over medium heat, heat the oil until it shimmers. Add the onion and cook, stirring occasionally, for about 5 minutes, or until softened. Stir in the garlic and cook for about 30 seconds more, then add the mushrooms. Continue to cook for about 5 minutes, or until the mushrooms begin to brown. Stir in the chili powder, cumin, and salt, then add the spinach and continue to cook, stirring occasionally, for about 1 minute, or until the spinach wilts. Stir in the beans and cook for about 3 more minutes, or until heated through.

4. Remove the tortillas from the oven and divide the vegetable mixture evenly among them. Top the filling in each burrito with a sprinkling of cheese and a dollop of salsa. Roll the tortillas around the filling, tucking in the sides to contain the filling. Serve hot.

Make it easier: Make a double batch, wrap each burrito tightly in a double layer of plastic wrap, and freeze them for later.

Crispy Sesame Tofu Wraps

Serves 4 / Prep time: 20 minutes / Cook time: 10 minutes

For this dish, tofu is glazed in a savory-sweet sauce of soy sauce, brown sugar, and rice vinegar and wrapped in a flour tortilla with shredded cabbage for crunch. The wraps are wonderful when the tofu is still warm but also delicious at room temperature, so you can pack them to go if you like.

1 (14-ounce) package extra-firm tofu, cut into 1-inch-thick slabs

¼ cup low-sodium soy sauce

¼ cup water

2 teaspoons brown sugar

1 teaspoon chile paste

1 garlic clove, minced

½ teaspoon rice vinegar

3 tablespoons cornstarch, divided

2 tablespoons cooking oil

2 teaspoons sesame oil

2 teaspoons toasted sesame seeds (optional)

4 flour tortillas

2 cups shredded cabbage

1. Lay the slabs of tofu in a single layer on a double layer of paper towels or a clean dish towel. Top with another double layer of paper towels or dish towel and then place something heavy on top (like a cast-iron skillet!). Let stand like this for about 15 minutes to squeeze excess water out of the tofu.

2. While the tofu is being pressed, in a small bowl, stir together the soy sauce, water, brown sugar, chile paste, garlic, vinegar, and 1 tablespoon of cornstarch.

3. Remove the weight and paper towels and pat the tofu dry. Cut the tofu into cubes.

4. In a large bowl, toss together the tofu cubes and remaining 2 tablespoons of cornstarch.

5. In a skillet over medium-high heat, heat the cooking oil and sesame oil together. Add the tofu and cook, turning occasionally, for about 7 minutes, or until the tofu is browned on all sides.

6. Add the sauce mixture to the skillet and continue to cook, stirring, until the sauce thickens and the tofu is well coated.

7. Remove the tofu from the skillet and toss with the sesame seeds (if using).

8. Wipe out the skillet and then heat the tortillas in it, one at a time, over medium-high heat.

9. Divide the tofu and cabbage among the tortillas and roll up like burritos. Serve immediately.

Make it easier: A tofu press makes it easy to squeeze the excess water out of tofu. This in turn enables the tofu to really soak up the flavorful sauce and also helps it cook up nice and crisp on the outside.

Black Bean and Quinoa Burgers

Serves 4 / **Prep time: 10 minutes** / **Cook time: 20 minutes**

These black bean and quinoa burgers really fill the bill when you're craving a burger. I love to top them with all the typical burger toppings, like sliced onion, pickles, tomatoes, crunchy lettuce, mayo, and ketchup. Serve these burgers with a side of fries or sweet potato fries for a perfect meal.

3 tablespoons olive oil, divided

½ onion, diced

1 large garlic clove, minced

1 (15-ounce) can black beans, drained and rinsed

1½ cups cooked quinoa

1 large egg

1 teaspoon chili powder

1 teaspoon ground cumin

½ teaspoon kosher salt

4 hamburger buns

1. In a skillet over medium-high heat, heat 2 table-spoons of oil. Add the onion and garlic and cook, stirring occasionally, for about 5 minutes, or until softened. Remove from the skillet and let cool.

2. In a large bowl, use a potato masher or the back of a large fork to mash the beans. Stir in the cooked onion and garlic, quinoa, egg, chili powder, cumin, and salt and mix to combine.

3. Using your hands, form the mixture into 4 patties, about 1 inch thick.

4. Wipe out the skillet, add the remaining 1 tablespoon of oil, and heat over medium-high heat. Cook the patties in the skillet for 4 to 5 minutes, or until golden brown on the bottom. Gently flip the burgers and cook for 3 to 4 more minutes, or until cooked through and browned on the second side.

5. Serve the burgers on the buns with your favorite burger toppings.

Variation tip: Add sliced cheese on top of the burgers as soon as you flip them. Then, cover the skillet while they cook on the second side, in order to melt the cheese.

Goat Cheese and Pesto Pizza

Serves 4 / **Prep time: 10 minutes** / **Cook time: 20 minutes**

The combination of herby basil pesto and tangy goat cheese with peppery arugula is simply divine. If you don't want to pull out your food processor or blender, substitute store-bought pesto for the homemade version.

FOR THE PESTO

¼ cup toasted pine nuts

2 ounces grated Parmesan cheese

1 garlic clove

½ teaspoon kosher salt

3 cups fresh basil leaves

6 tablespoons extra-virgin olive oil

FOR THE PIZZAS

1 pound fresh pizza dough, split into 2 equal pieces

1 (5.5-ounce) log soft fresh goat cheese

4 cups arugula leaves

TO MAKE THE PESTO

1. In a food processor or blender, combine the pine nuts, cheese, garlic, and salt and pulse until the nuts are finely ground. Add the basil and process to chop finely. With the motor running, add the oil in a slow stream. Process until the pesto is smooth.

TO MAKE THE PIZZAS

2. Place a skillet in the oven and preheat the oven to 450°F.

3. While the skillet and oven are preheating, press or roll one of the pieces of dough into a circle roughly the size of the skillet.

4. Remove the skillet from the oven and place the dough in it. Spread half of the pesto on top, then top with half of the goat cheese.

5. Return the skillet to the oven and bake, rotating halfway through, for 10 to 12 minutes, or until the crust is golden brown and crisp.

6. Transfer the cooked pizza to a cutting board, slice, and garnish with half of the arugula to serve. Repeat with the second pizza.

Cast-iron tip: Preheating the skillet that you'll cook the pizza in ensures that the pizza cooks quickly and evenly.

Spanish Tortilla with Manchego Cheese and Smoked Paprika Aioli

Serves **4 to 6** / Prep time: **10 minutes** / Cook time: **15 minutes**

Spanish tortilla is similar to a frittata or a crustless quiche. It's often served as an appetizer or snack in Spain. A true tortilla is made with eggs, onions, and potatoes and cooked in copious amounts of olive oil. A well-seasoned cast-iron skillet is perfect for cooking this dish because the nonstick finish allows the tortilla to slide out easily. The high heat of the cast iron also makes for a deep, golden-brown crust.

½ onion, diced

1 medium potato, peeled and diced

¾ teaspoon kosher salt

⅓ cup olive oil

5 large eggs

4 ounces Manchego cheese, diced small

½ cup diced roasted red peppers (from a jar, drained)

½ cup mayonnaise

2 teaspoons smoked paprika

1. Set a sieve over a heat-safe bowl.

2. In a skillet, combine the onion, potato, salt, and oil and heat over medium-high heat. Cook, stirring occasionally, for about 7 minutes, or until the potato and onion are softened and beginning to brown. Pour the mixture into the prepared sieve, reserving the oil.

3. In a medium bowl, whisk the eggs. Stir in the cheese. Add the potato mixture and peppers and toss to combine everything well.

4. Return 3 to 4 tablespoons of the reserved oil to the skillet and heat over medium-high heat. Add the potato-and-egg mixture and cook for about 5 minutes, or until the bottom begins to brown and the top is beginning to set.

5. Set a plate or platter over the skillet and, holding the plate firmly on top of the skillet, invert it to release the tortilla onto the plate. Slide the tortilla back into the skillet so that what was the top is now the bottom. Continue to cook for about 3 more minutes, or until the bottom is browned and the center is set.

6. While the tortilla is cooking, stir together the mayonnaise and paprika in a small bowl.

7. Slide the finished tortilla onto a platter. To serve, slice into wedges and top with a dollop of the aioli.

Cast-iron tip: To successfully and safely flip your tortilla, be sure to use very sturdy, thick oven mitts. I use the mitten type made out of silicone so that I can safely handle the very hot skillet.

Pumpkin Mac and Cheese

Serves 4 / **Prep time: 15 minutes** / **Cook time: 15 minutes**

You have to use an extra pot to boil the pasta for this recipe, but it's totally worth it. It's an ooey, gooey, crispy-crusted mac and cheese recipe with pureed pumpkin stirred in for extra flavor, color, and nutrition. I like to use sharp white Cheddar or Gruyère for this recipe because of their strong flavors and good melting abilities, but you can use your favorite or a combination of two or more cheeses.

1 (12-ounce) package macaroni

1 tablespoon unsalted butter, plus 4 tablespoons (½ stick) melted

1½ cups milk (low-fat or whole, not nonfat)

1 teaspoon dry mustard

½ teaspoon ground paprika

½ teaspoon kosher salt

2½ cups (about 10 ounces) grated cheese(s) of your choice, divided

4 to 5 tablespoons all-purpose flour

1 (15-ounce) can pumpkin puree

1½ cups panko bread crumbs

1. Preheat the broiler.

2. Cook the pasta according to the package directions and then drain well.

3. While the pasta cooks, heat a skillet over low heat. Add 1 tablespoon of butter. When the butter becomes foamy and begins to brown, whisk in the milk, mustard, paprika, and salt.

4. Add 2 cups of grated cheese to the skillet, about ½ cup at a time, whisking after each addition. When the cheese melts completely, sift the flour into the sauce, 1 tablespoon at a time, whisking after each addition, until the mixture thickens. Stir in the pumpkin puree.

5. Add the cooked pasta to the sauce, stirring to coat well, and remove the skillet from the heat.

6. In a medium bowl, mix well to combine the remaining ½ cup of cheese, the bread crumbs, and the remaining 4 tablespoons of melted butter. Sprinkle the mixture evenly over the top of the pasta.

7. Put the skillet under the broiler and cook, watching carefully so that it doesn't burn, for about 5 minutes, or until the top is browned and bubbly. Serve hot.

Cast-iron tip: If the gooey mac and cheese sticks to your skillet, don't fret. Fill the skillet with a couple of inches of water and bring it to a boil over medium-high heat. This will soften the stuck-on food. Use a stiff spatula, if needed, to scrape off any stubborn bits, then clean the skillet as usual.

Skillet-Roasted Feta and Tomatoes with Pasta

Serves 4 / **Prep time: 5 minutes** / **Cook time: 25 minutes**

Toss tomatoes, garlic, herbs, and feta cheese into a skillet. Roast them in the oven, and they turn into a flavorful pasta sauce with zero fuss. A version of this recipe became an internet sensation, and it's not hard to see why. It's one of the easiest ways to get a scrumptious dinner on the table fast.

1½ pounds cherry tomatoes or grape tomatoes

2 garlic cloves, minced

1 tablespoon fresh oregano leaves

4 tablespoons olive oil, divided

1 (8-ounce) block feta cheese

Kosher salt

Freshly ground black pepper

8 ounces uncooked pasta (fusilli, penne, rotelle, or another short pasta)

Grated Parmesan cheese, for garnish

Fresh basil, julienned, for garnish (optional)

1. Preheat the oven to 450°F.

2. Put the tomatoes, garlic, and oregano in a skillet and add 3 tablespoons of oil. Toss until all the tomatoes are coated with oil.

3. Move the tomatoes to the side of the skillet to make space and then place the feta in the space. Drizzle the remaining 1 tablespoon of oil over the feta. Season everything with salt and pepper.

4. Bake for 25 minutes, or until the tomatoes have burst open, the cheese is melty and browned on top, and the whole thing is sizzling and bubbling.

5. While the cheese and tomatoes are in the oven, cook the pasta according to the package directions and then drain, reserving ½ cup of the cooking water.

6. Remove the skillet from the oven. Using a spoon, break up the cheese a bit and then toss everything together to combine well. Add the pasta to the skillet and mix well, adding a bit of the pasta cooking water if needed.

7. Serve immediately, garnished with the Parmesan and the fresh basil (if using).

Cast-iron tip: Because this dish is heavy on tomatoes, which are acidic, make sure you have a really good seasoning coat on your skillet before cooking it, or you may end up with a metallic-tasting sauce.

Stir-Fried Rice Noodles with Tofu and Broccoli

Serves 4 / **Prep time: 10 minutes** / **Cook time: 20 minutes**

This quick noodle-and-vegetable dinner is a simplified version of the popular Thai street food called *pad see ew*. You can add other vegetables if you want to make it more filling—and strips of red bell pepper would add a nice splash of color.

¼ cup low-sodium soy sauce

2 tablespoons hoisin sauce

1 tablespoon brown sugar

2 tablespoons cooking oil

2 garlic cloves, minced

1 shallot, diced

1 (14-ounce) block firm tofu, cubed

1 cup broccoli florets

1 (16-ounce) package wide, flat dried rice noodles, soaked according to package directions

2 scallions, thinly sliced, for garnish (optional)

1. In a small bowl, stir together the soy sauce, hoisin sauce, and brown sugar.

2. In a skillet over high heat, heat the oil.

3. Add the garlic and shallot and cook, stirring occasionally, for 1 minute, or until the shallot begins to soften. Add the tofu and cook, stirring occasionally, for about 5 minutes, or until it begins to brown on all sides. Add the broccoli florets and cook, stirring, for about 7 minutes, or until the broccoli is tender.

4. Add the noodles and the sauce mixture to the pan and cook, tossing the noodles around to mix everything together, for 3 to 5 minutes, or until the sauce begins to bubble and thicken. Serve hot, garnished with the scallions (if using).

Variation tip: If you aren't vegan, you can add eggs to this dish. Before cooking the garlic and shallots, heat a bit of oil in the skillet. Add 2 beaten eggs and cook for about 2 minutes, or until just set. Remove the eggs from the pan and cut into pieces. Return the cooked egg to the pan along with the sauce mixture in step 4.

Chickpea and Potato Curry

Serves **4** / Prep time: **10 minutes** / Cook time: **20 minutes**

This hearty stew of chickpeas and potatoes is a filling one-skillet meal. Garam masala is a mixture of spices—usually a combination of black and white peppercorns, cloves, cinnamon, nutmeg, mace, black and green cardamom, bay leaves, and cumin—that is used in the cuisines of India and Pakistan. Using store-bought spice mixtures like this one is a great way to get lots of flavor with just a few ingredients.

1 tablespoon coconut or extra-virgin olive oil

1 onion, diced

1 jalapeño pepper, minced (seeded for a less spicy kick)

3 garlic cloves, minced

1 tablespoon minced peeled fresh ginger (about a 1-inch piece)

1½ teaspoons garam masala

1 teaspoon ground cumin

1 teaspoon kosher salt

2 large russet potatoes, peeled and diced

10 to 12 kale leaves, ribbed, leaves julienned

1 (28-ounce) can diced tomatoes with their juices

1 (15-ounce) can chickpeas (or 1½ cups cooked chickpeas), drained and rinsed

1. In a skillet over medium heat, heat the oil until it begins to shimmer. Reduce the heat to medium and add the onion, jalapeño, garlic, and ginger. Cook, stirring frequently, for about 5 minutes, or until the onion softens. Add the garam masala, cumin, and salt. Continue to cook, stirring, for 1 more minute.

2. Add the potatoes and kale and cook, stirring, for about 1 minute, or until the kale begins to wilt. Add the tomatoes and their juices and stir to mix.

3. Increase the heat to medium-high, stir in the chickpeas, and bring to a boil. Reduce the heat to medium and let simmer, uncovered and stirring occasionally, for 10 to 12 minutes, or until the potatoes are tender. Serve hot.

Variation tip: If you want a richer sauce, stir in some heavy cream or coconut milk while the sauce is simmering in step 3.

Pinto Bean Chili

Serves 4 / Prep time: **5 minutes** / Cook time: **25 minutes**

Chili is such a satisfying meal, and this skillet version is quick, easy, and full of flavor. Serve this chili with a side of Cheesy Jalapeño Corn Bread (page 42) or top it with your favorite toppings, like sour cream, shredded cheese, salsa, and tortilla chips.

2 tablespoons olive oil

1 onion, diced

2 garlic cloves, minced

1 tablespoon chili powder

1 teaspoon paprika

1 teaspoon ground cumin

2 (15-ounce) cans pinto beans, drained and rinsed

1 (15-ounce) can diced tomatoes with their juices

1 teaspoon kosher salt

¼ cup chopped fresh cilantro

1. In a skillet over medium-high heat, heat the oil. Add the onion and cook, stirring occasionally, for about 5 minutes, or until softened. Stir in the garlic, chili powder, paprika, and cumin. Add the beans, tomatoes and their juices, and salt and bring to a boil. Reduce the heat to low and simmer, stirring occasionally, for 15 to 20 minutes, or until the liquid thickens.

2. Serve hot, garnished with the cilantro.

Cast-iron tip: Chili is one of those dishes that are even better the day after you make it, but don't store it in your skillet overnight. After cooking, let the chili cool to room temperature, transfer it to a storage container, and then refrigerate it overnight. Reheat the chili in the skillet, in a saucepan, or in the microwave.

White Bean Stew with Greens and Tomatoes

Serves 4 / Prep time: **5 minutes** / Cook time: **25 minutes**

This quick stovetop vegan stew is simple but super satisfying. This stew makes a healthy and filling one-pan meal. Serve the stew with hunks of crusty bread for scooping and dunking.

1 tablespoon extra-virgin olive oil

1 onion, diced

3 garlic cloves, minced

8 ounces kale, ribbed, leaves julienned

¾ teaspoon kosher salt

1 (28-ounce) can diced tomatoes with their juices

½ cup vegetable broth

2 (15.5-ounce) cans cannellini beans, drained and rinsed

1 tablespoon minced fresh oregano leaves, or 1 teaspoon crumbled dried oregano

Freshly ground black pepper

Pinch red pepper flakes (optional)

1. In a skillet over medium heat, heat the oil. Add the onion and cook, stirring frequently, for about 5 minutes, or until soft and translucent. Stir in the garlic and cook, stirring, for 1 minute. Add the kale and salt and cook, stirring occasionally, for about 5 more minutes, or until the kale is tender.

2. Increase the heat to high and add the tomatoes and their juices, broth, beans, and oregano. Season with black pepper and red pepper flakes (if using). Bring to a boil, then reduce the heat to medium-low and simmer for 10 minutes. Serve hot.

Variation tip: If you are not vegan, top the stew with shredded Gruyère cheese and place the skillet under the broiler for a few minutes until the cheese is melted, bubbly, and golden brown.

Veggie Enchilada Skillet Casserole

Serves 4 / **Prep time: 5 minutes** / **Cook time: 25 minutes**

These plant-based enchiladas are loaded with black beans and sautéed veggies. The easy-to-make homemade tomatillo sauce makes the dish extra special, too. Top the enchiladas with your favorite vegan cheese (or regular cheese for a vegetarian version). Feel free to add whatever toppings you like. I love a dollop of guacamole and a few shakes of hot sauce.

1½ pounds fresh tomatillos, husked

3 garlic cloves, minced, divided

1 jalapeño pepper, seeded for a milder version

¼ cup fresh cilantro

1 teaspoon ground cumin

1½ teaspoons kosher salt, divided

¾ teaspoon freshly ground black pepper, divided

3 tablespoons olive oil, divided

1 onion, diced

2 bell peppers (any color), diced

2 (15-ounce) cans black beans, drained and rinsed

8 corn tortillas

1 cup shredded vegan cheese

1. Preheat the oven to 450°F.

2. In a blender or food processor, combine the tomatillos, 2 garlic cloves, jalapeño, cilantro, cumin, 1 teaspoon of salt, and ½ teaspoon of pepper. Process until smooth.

3. In a skillet over medium-high heat, heat 2 tablespoons of oil until it shimmers. Add the onion and bell peppers and cook, stirring, for about 5 minutes, or until softened. Stir in the remaining 1 garlic clove, remaining ½ teaspoon of salt, and remaining ¼ teaspoon of pepper. Stir in the beans and half of the sauce and cook, stirring, for about 2 minutes, or until the sauce is bubbling and the beans are heated through. Transfer the mixture to a bowl and wipe out the skillet.

4. Add the remaining 1 tablespoon of oil to the skillet and use a paper towel to spread it over the bottom.

5. Spread a couple of heaping spoonfuls of sauce over the bottom of the skillet and then make a single layer of tortillas to cover the bottom, tearing the tortillas into pieces as necessary to fill in gaps. Spoon half of the vegetable-and-bean mixture on top and spread into an even layer. Top with another layer of tortillas, another layer of filling, and then a final layer of tortillas. Pour the remaining sauce over the top. Sprinkle the cheese on top.

6. Bake for about 15 minutes, or until the sauce is bubbling and the cheese is melted. Serve hot.

Variation tip: If you don't have fresh tomatillos, you can use 1 (28-ounce) can of tomatillos, drained, instead.

Kimchi Fried Rice

Serves 4 / **Prep time: 5 minutes** / **Cook time: 15 minutes**

Kimchi adds crunch and a burst of spicy, tangy flavor to this quick stir-fried rice. Fried rice is a great way to use up leftovers. I often make extra rice just so I can have some in the refrigerator for fried rice. Using leftover rice here is necessary because the rice needs time to dry out, or the grains will become mushy and clump together when fried. If you want to make this dish even more filling, add a fried egg on top of each serving.

2 tablespoons vegetable oil

2 carrots, diced

3 cups leftover cooked rice

1 cup chopped vegan kimchi, plus ¼ cup juice from the jar

1½ cups cooked frozen edamame

¼ cup soy sauce

1. In a 12-inch skillet over medium-high heat, heat the oil until it shimmers. Add the carrots and cook, stirring occasionally, for about 5 minutes, or until tender.

2. Add the rice to the skillet, breaking it up with a spatula. Cook, stirring occasionally, until the rice is hot and beginning to brown a bit on the bottom. Add the kimchi and edamame and cook, stirring, for 2 to 3 minutes, or until well incorporated and heated through.

3. In a small bowl, stir together the soy sauce and kimchi juice. Add the sauce mixture to the rice in the skillet and continue to cook, stirring, for about 2 more minutes, or until well incorporated. Serve hot.

Make it easier: When you put cold leftover rice into the skillet, it will tend to stick together in a big clump. Wet your hands with cold water and break up the clumps with your hands as you add the rice to the skillet.

CHAPTER 5

FISH AND SEAFOOD

Olive Oil–Poached Salmon and Baby Spinach Salad, page 70

Pan-Roasted Fish with Cherry Tomatoes, Bell Pepper, and Mint

Serves 4 / **Prep time:** **10 minutes** / **Cook time:** **20 minutes**

For this quick meal, mild white fish (you can use anything from cod to snapper, halibut, or tilapia) is roasted in the skillet with tomatoes, peppers, shallot, and garlic. A bit of white wine and butter make for spoon-worthy pan juices that you'll want to sop up with some good bread.

2 tablespoons olive oil

1 shallot, thinly sliced

2 garlic cloves, minced

1 pint cherry tomatoes, halved

1 large bell pepper (any color), seeded and thinly sliced

1½ teaspoons kosher salt, divided

¼ cup dry white wine

4 (6-ounce) white fish fillets

½ teaspoon freshly ground black pepper

2 tablespoons unsalted butter, cut into small pieces

1 teaspoon grated lemon zest (from about ½ lemon)

¼ cup chopped fresh mint

1. Preheat the oven to 400°F.

2. In a skillet over medium-high heat, heat the oil until it shimmers. Add the shallot and cook, stirring frequently, for about 3 minutes, or until it begins to soften. Stir in the garlic and cook for 30 seconds more. Add the tomatoes, bell pepper, and ½ teaspoon of salt and cook, stirring, for about 3 more minutes, or until the tomatoes just begin to break down and the pepper begins to soften. Add the wine and cook, stirring, for 2 more minutes, or until the liquid is reduced by about half. Remove the skillet from the heat.

3. Season the fish with the remaining 1 teaspoon of salt and the pepper and lay the fillets in the skillet, nestling them into the vegetables. Scatter the butter pieces and lemon zest over the fish and spoon a bit of the vegetables and liquid over the top.

4. Transfer the skillet to the oven and roast for about 10 minutes, or until the fish is cooked through and flakes easily with a fork.

5. Serve immediately, garnished with the mint.

Spicy Shrimp and Grits with Green Beans

Serves 4 / **Prep time: 5 minutes** / **Cook time: 25 minutes**

This one-skillet version of the classic Southern dish makes a great 30-minute meal. The shrimp and grits are cooked in the skillet together. Blanch some green beans in boiling water while the grits are in the oven, and you've got dinner ready to go.

3½ cups water

½ cup heavy (whipping) cream

2 tablespoons unsalted butter

1 teaspoon kosher salt

1 cup grits (not instant)

1½ cups (about 6 ounces) shredded extra-sharp white Cheddar cheese, divided

3 large eggs, lightly beaten

½ teaspoon cayenne pepper

1½ pounds peeled and deveined large shrimp

8 ounces green beans

2 scallions, thinly sliced

1. Preheat the oven to 450°F.

2. In a skillet over medium heat, combine the water, heavy cream, butter, and salt and bring to a boil. Whisk in the grits in a steady stream. Adjust the heat to low, and cook, stirring frequently, for about 10 minutes, or until the grits are creamy. Remove the skillet from the heat.

3. In a medium bowl, whisk 1 cup of cheese with the eggs and cayenne. Stir the egg-and-cheese mixture into the grits. Add the shrimp and cover with the mixture. Sprinkle the remaining ½ cup of cheese over the top.

4. Bake for about 15 minutes, or until the cheese melts and browns, and the shrimp are pink.

5. Meanwhile, bring a medium saucepan of salted water to a boil. Add the green beans and cook for 3 to 4 minutes, or until tender. Drain.

6. Remove the skillet from the oven and let stand for a few minutes before serving the shrimp and grits garnished with the scallions, with the green beans on the side.

Olive Oil-Poached Salmon and Baby Spinach Salad

Serves 4 / **Prep time: 10 minutes** / **Cook time: 15 minutes**

Poaching salmon in olive oil keeps it moist, and it also helps the fish retain all of its rich flavor. The fatty fish is counterbalanced by the crisp spinach leaves and tart lemon vinaigrette. Toasted pecans add a bit of crunch.

4 (6-ounce) salmon fillets

1½ teaspoons kosher salt, divided

¾ teaspoon freshly ground black pepper, divided

2 cups extra-virgin olive oil, plus 2 tablespoons

10 ounces baby spinach leaves

1 pint grape tomatoes, halved

3 tablespoons freshly squeezed lemon juice

¼ cup toasted pecans

1. Preheat the oven to 250°F.

2. Season the salmon fillets with 1 teaspoon of salt and ½ teaspoon of pepper.

3. In a skillet over medium heat, heat 2 cups of oil until it is warm but not hot. Add the salmon fillets to the oil, skin-side down.

4. Transfer the skillet to the oven and bake for 12 to 14 minutes, or until the salmon is just barely cooked through. Remove the skillet from the oven and let the fish rest in the oil for about 15 minutes.

5. Meanwhile, in a medium bowl, toss together the spinach and tomatoes.

6. In a small bowl, whisk together the remaining 2 tablespoons of oil, the lemon juice, the remaining ½ teaspoon of salt, and the remaining ¼ teaspoon of pepper.

7. Add the vinaigrette to the bowl with the spinach and tomatoes and toss to coat.

8. Remove the fish from the skillet and drain it briefly on a paper towel-lined plate. Remove and discard the skin from each salmon fillet.

9. Divide the salad among 4 serving plates. Top each with a salmon fillet. Garnish with the pecans and serve immediately.

Variation tip: You can substitute another meaty fish, cod or halibut, for example, for the salmon.

Stuffed Baked Trout

Serves **4** / Prep time: **5 minutes** / Cook time: **25 minutes**

Fresh fish stuffed with a simple bread crumb stuffing is one of those meals that seems fancy but is surprisingly easy to make. If you have any fresh herbs—dill, basil, sage, thyme, chives—chop up a couple of tablespoons and add them to the stuffing mixture before stuffing the fish.

4 tablespoons (½ stick) unsalted butter

1 shallot, diced

1 cup soft bread crumbs

1 teaspoon kosher salt, divided

½ teaspoon freshly ground black pepper

4 whole trout

1. Preheat the oven to 400°F.

2. In a skillet over medium-high heat, melt the butter. Add the shallot and cook, stirring occasionally, for about 5 minutes, or until softened.

3. Remove the skillet from the heat and stir in the bread crumbs, ½ teaspoon of salt, and the pepper.

4. Season the inside of the trout with the remaining ½ teaspoon of salt. Divide the stuffing among the fish, filling each trout. Arrange the fish in the skillet in a single layer. Bake for about 20 minutes, or until the fish is cooked and flakes easily with a fork.Remove the fish from the skillet, placing them on serving plates.

5. Serve immediately.

Variation tip: Serve this with a side of cooked chard. Heat 1 tablespoon of olive oil over medium-high heat, and cook the chard with a pinch of salt and black pepper for 3 minutes, or until the chard wilts.

Shrimp with Basil and Feta over Pasta

Serves **4** / Prep time: **10 minutes** / Cook time: **15 minutes**

This quick pasta dinner is a favorite on summer nights. I love the combination of the fresh basil, feta, and tomatoes, but you could substitute another fresh herb, such as mint, if you like. For even more flavor, you can sauté a diced onion or shallot in the skillet before adding the tomatoes.

12 ounces dried short pasta, such as fusilli or rotelle

3 tablespoons extra-virgin olive oil, divided

1 pound peeled and deveined large shrimp

¾ teaspoon kosher salt, divided

½ teaspoon freshly ground black pepper, divided

3 cups halved cherry tomatoes (about 1 pound)

1 cup crumbled feta cheese

1 cup fresh basil leaves, torn

1. Cook the pasta according to the package directions, then drain and place in a large bowl with 1 tablespoon of oil. Toss to coat.

2. While the pasta cooks, in a skillet over medium heat, heat the remaining 2 tablespoons of oil. Add the shrimp, ½ teaspoon of salt, and ¼ teaspoon of pepper and cook, stirring, for about 3 minutes, or until the shrimp are opaque and just cooked through. Transfer the shrimp to a plate.

3. Add the tomatoes and the remaining ¼ teaspoon of salt and ¼ teaspoon of pepper to the skillet and cook, stirring occasionally, for about 5 minutes, or until the tomatoes begin to blister and break down a bit. Return the shrimp to the skillet and cook for about 1 more minute, just to heat through.

4. Add the shrimp and tomatoes to the pasta and toss to mix. Add the feta and basil and toss again. Serve immediately.

Variation tip: This dish would work just as well with any mild white fish. Cut the fish into 2-inch pieces and cook it the same way you would cook the shrimp.

Fish Tacos with Cilantro Lime Slaw

Serves **4** / Prep time: **10 minutes** / Cook time: **10 minutes**

This is one of my favorite skillet dinners because it's so quick and easy to make while still being light and healthy. This meal is perfect for weeknight dinners when you need to get something nutritious on the table fast. Add whatever garnishes you like on your tacos—avocado slices, guacamole, thinly sliced radishes or scallions, or pico de gallo salsa.

8 (6-inch) corn tortillas

2 cups thinly shredded cabbage

1 jalapeño pepper, minced (seeded for less spiciness)

2 tablespoons freshly squeezed lime juice

2 tablespoons minced fresh cilantro

¾ teaspoon kosher salt

Pinch freshly ground black pepper

1½ teaspoons brown sugar

1½ tablespoons chili powder

4 (6-ounce) cod fillets

1 tablespoon cooking oil

1. Preheat the oven to 450°F.

2. Wrap the tortillas in aluminum foil and heat them in the oven while you prepare the rest of the dish.

3. In a medium bowl, toss together the cabbage, jalapeño, lime juice, cilantro, salt, and pepper.

4. Sprinkle the brown sugar and chili powder over the fish, coating both sides of each fillet.

5. In a skillet over medium-high heat, heat the oil until it begins to shimmer. Add the fish and cook for about 3 minutes per side, or until cooked through and lightly browned.

6. Remove the tortillas from the oven and place 2 on each serving plate, overlapping. Place a fish fillet on top of each stack of tortillas. Top with a handful of slaw. Serve immediately.

Variation tip: You can use any white fish for this dish. If you don't have cod, try sole, tilapia, catfish, or snapper.

Braised Cod with Olives and Tomatoes

Serves 4 / Prep time: **10 minutes** / Cook time: **10 minutes**

Cod is a mild-flavored but meaty-fleshed fish that is perfect for oven-roasting. You can substitute another white fish, such as halibut, if you can't find cod. Green olives give this dish tons of flavor, providing a rich counterpoint to the acidic tomatoes.

4 tablespoons extra-virgin olive oil, divided

6 canned plum tomatoes, drained and coarsely chopped

½ red onion, sliced

1 cup pitted green olives

¼ cup capers

1 garlic clove, minced

⅛ teaspoon red pepper flakes

Kosher salt

Freshly ground black pepper

1¼ pounds (¾-inch-thick) cod fillets

¼ cup chopped fresh flat-leaf parsley

1. Preheat the oven to 400°F.

2. Coat the bottom of a skillet with 3 tablespoons of oil. Add the tomatoes, onion, olives, capers, garlic, and red pepper flakes to the skillet and mix. Season with salt and pepper. Cover the skillet with a lid and set it over medium-high heat, bringing the mixture to a simmer.

3. Pat the fish dry with paper towels, season both sides of the fillets with salt and pepper, and add them to the skillet in a single layer over the tomato mixture. Drizzle the remaining 1 tablespoon of oil over the fish. Transfer the skillet to the oven and cook, uncovered, for about 8 minutes, or until the fish is cooked through and flakes easily with a fork. Garnish with parsley and serve hot.

Variation tip: To make this a one-skillet meal, add 1½ pounds of thinly sliced potatoes on top of the tomatoes. Cover the skillet and set it over medium-low heat. Simmer without stirring for 20 minutes, or until the potatoes begin to soften. Uncover the skillet, add the fish, and roast, uncovered, until the fish is done.

Seared Scallops with Peas and Bacon

Serves 4 / Prep time: **10 minutes** / Cook time: **20 minutes**

Scallops are best when quickly seared on the outside to lock in their juices. A cast-iron skillet is the perfect pan for this purpose. Get the pan very hot, then add the scallops and cook for 2 to 3 minutes per side, browning them quickly. Peas, bacon, and lemon are all perfect partners for the sweet, meaty scallops.

4 thick-cut bacon slices, cut into ¼-inch matchsticks

3 tablespoons unsalted butter, divided

16 large sea scallops (about 1½ pounds), patted very dry with paper towels

Kosher salt

Freshly ground black pepper

½ small onion, diced

2 cups fresh or frozen (thawed) peas

¼ cup chicken or vegetable broth

1 teaspoon freshly squeezed lemon juice

2 tablespoons finely chopped fresh flat-leaf parsley

1. Heat a skillet over medium-high heat. Add the bacon and cook, stirring frequently, for about 4 minutes, or until browned and crisp. Using a slotted spoon, transfer the bacon to a paper towel–lined plate.

2. Discard the excess bacon fat, leaving about 1 tablespoon in the skillet. Add 1 tablespoon of butter. Heat over medium-high heat until the butter is melted.

3. Season the scallops with salt and pepper. Reduce the heat to medium and add the scallops to the skillet. Cook for 2 to 3 minutes on each side, or until nicely browned on both the top and bottom and just cooked through. Transfer the scallops to a plate.

4. Add the remaining 2 tablespoons of butter to the skillet, and when it is melted, add the onion. Cook, stirring frequently, for about 5 minutes, or until the onion is softened. Stir in the peas and broth and cook for about 2 more minutes, or just until heated through. Stir in the lemon juice, parsley, and bacon. Add the scallops and let cook for about 1 more minute, or until heated through. Serve immediately.

Variation tip: This dish uses large sea scallops. If you can't find those, you can substitute bay scallops. They're much smaller, so they'll cook faster. Cook them, stirring frequently, for just about 3 minutes.

Spicy Stir-Fried Kung Pao Shrimp

Serves 4 / Prep time: **10 minutes** / Cook time: **10 minutes**

Plump shrimp are quickly stir-fried with chiles and peanuts for a dish that is loaded with flavor. A cast-iron skillet is ideal for toasting the chiles and infusing their oil with their flavor. It's also perfect for quickly searing the shrimp.

¼ cup soy sauce

¼ cup water

1 teaspoon rice vinegar

1 teaspoon cornstarch

1 teaspoon sugar

2 tablespoons vegetable oil

5 to 10 small dried red chiles

1 (2-inch) piece ginger, peeled and thinly sliced

1¼ pounds peeled and deveined large shrimp

½ cup roasted peanuts

4 scallions, white and light green parts only, thinly sliced

1. In a small bowl, stir together the soy sauce, water, vinegar, cornstarch, and sugar.

2. In a skillet over high heat, heat the oil until it begins to shimmer. Add the chiles and cook, stirring, for about 1 minute, or until they become aromatic. Add the ginger, shrimp, and peanuts and continue to cook, stirring frequently, for about 4 minutes, or until the shrimp are cooked through.

3. Add the sauce mixture and cook, stirring, for 2 to 3 more minutes, or until the sauce thickens.

4. Stir in the scallions and serve immediately.

Variation tip: If you want to add some vegetables to this stir-fry, slice a bell pepper or two (any color) into strips and sauté it in the skillet for about 5 minutes, or until tender, before adding the shrimp.

Butter and Garlic Steamed Mussels

Serves 4 / Prep time: 10 minutes / Cook time: 15 minutes

Mussels are a great option when you want to make something that seems a little fancy but is still affordable and easy to prepare. This simple recipe relies on the classic flavors of butter, garlic, wine, parsley, and lemon. The broth is so delicious, you'll want to serve hunks of crusty bread alongside for dunking.

4 tablespoons (½ stick) unsalted butter

1 small onion, diced

4 garlic cloves, minced

½ teaspoon red pepper flakes

¾ cup dry white wine

2 pounds live mussels in their shells, scrubbed and rinsed

Juice of 1 lemon

3 tablespoons chopped fresh flat-leaf parsley

1. In a skillet over medium-high heat, melt the butter. Add the onion and cook, stirring occasionally, for about 5 minutes, or until softened. Add the garlic and red pepper flakes and cook, stirring, for about 15 seconds, or just until fragrant. Add the wine and bring to a simmer.

2. Add the mussels to the skillet and stir to coat. Cover the skillet and cook for 5 to 7 minutes, or until most of the mussels open. Discard any mussels that don't open.

3. Remove the cover and stir in the lemon juice and parsley. Serve immediately.

Cast-iron tip: The mussels are cooked by steaming them in the broth mixture. If you don't have a lid for your skillet, use a large lid from another skillet or pot. If you don't have a large enough lid, use a piece of aluminum foil. Press the foil on with oven mitt–protected hands.

Shrimp Po' Boy Sandwiches

Serves **4** / Prep time: **10 minutes** / Cook time: **15 minutes**

The Shrimp Po' Boy is a classic New Orleans sandwich. This is a simplified version, but it is still spicy and delicious. Shrimp are dredged in a spiced flour-and-cornmeal coating and then fried until crispy. Then they're piled on sandwich rolls that have been slathered with a quick remoulade sauce and topped with crunchy shredded lettuce.

Cooking oil, for frying

1 cup all-purpose flour

1 cup cornmeal

1½ tablespoons Creole seasoning (such as Tony Chachere's)

1½ pounds peeled and deveined shrimp

1 cup buttermilk

½ cup mayonnaise

2 tablespoons sweet pickle relish

1 tablespoon hot sauce (such as Crystal or Tabasco)

4 sandwich rolls, split

2 cups shredded lettuce

1. Fill a skillet with about 2 inches of oil and heat over medium-high heat.

2. In a wide, shallow bowl, stir together the flour, cornmeal, and Creole seasoning.

3. In a large bowl, toss together the shrimp and buttermilk until the shrimp are well coated. Dredge the shrimp in the flour mixture.

4. When the oil is shimmering, drop the dredged shrimp into it in batches, without crowding the skillet. Fry for 3 to 4 minutes, or until golden brown all over. Transfer to paper towels to drain and repeat with the remaining shrimp.

5. In a small bowl, stir together the mayonnaise, relish, and hot sauce. Spread this mixture on the split sandwich rolls. Add the shrimp to each roll and top with the lettuce. Serve immediately.

Cast-iron tip: Use a 10-inch skillet for this recipe if you have one, so you won't need to use too much oil.

POULTRY

Crispy Fried Chicken Strips, page 87

Seared Chicken Breast Sandwiches with Avocado and Greens

Serves 4 / **Prep time: 5 minutes, plus 15 minutes to marinate** / **Cook time: 10 minutes**

Chicken breast fillets take on lots of flavor and get nice and tender with just a quick marinade in olive oil and lemon juice. Sear the chicken quickly in a hot skillet and then pile it onto French rolls with avocado and greens.

3 tablespoons olive oil, divided

Juice of 1 lemon

¾ teaspoon kosher salt

2 boneless, skinless chicken breasts, sliced horizontally to make 4 thin fillets

4 French rolls, split

1 avocado, mashed

2 tablespoons Dijon mustard

1 large tomato, sliced

1½ cups arugula or baby spinach leaves

1. In a medium bowl, combine 2 tablespoons of oil, the lemon juice, and the salt. Add the chicken and toss to coat. Set aside for 15 minutes to marinate.

2. In a skillet over medium-high heat, heat the remaining 1 tablespoon of oil until it shimmers. Add the chicken to the skillet, discarding the marinade, and cook for 4 to 5 minutes, or until the bottom is golden brown. Flip the chicken and cook for about 3 more minutes, or until golden brown and cooked through. Remove the chicken from the skillet and let cool for a couple of minutes.

3. Spread about 1½ teaspoons of mustard and one-fourth of the avocado on the bottom half of each roll. Place 1 chicken breast fillet on each roll and top with the tomato slices and greens. Cover with the top half of the rolls. Serve immediately.

Cast-iron tip: Let the chicken breasts sear undisturbed until the bottoms are golden brown. Once they're properly seared, they'll release easily from the pan without sticking.

Greek-Style Turkey Burgers

Serves 4 / Prep time: 15 minutes / Cook time: 10 minutes

Fresh herbs and tangy feta cheese give these burgers tons of flavor. Cooking the burgers in a cast-iron skillet gives them a golden-brown sear on the outside that seals in all of their delicious juices. Top these burgers with a yogurt tzatziki (stir together Greek yogurt, garlic, fresh herbs like parsley and chives, salt, pepper, and a squirt of lemon juice) or your favorite burger condiments.

1½ pounds ground turkey

¾ cup (about 4 ounces) crumbled feta cheese

1 small red onion, minced

1 garlic clove, minced

¼ cup finely chopped fresh mint

1 teaspoon ground cumin

1 teaspoon kosher salt

½ teaspoon freshly ground black pepper

1 tablespoon olive oil

4 burger buns, split

4 lettuce leaves

4 thin tomato slices

1. In a medium bowl, combine the turkey, feta, onion, garlic, mint, cumin, salt, and pepper. Using your hands, mix gently until well combined. Shape the mixture into 4 patties, each about ½ inch thick.

2. In a skillet over medium-high heat, heat the oil. Add the burgers and cook for 4 to 5 minutes, or until nicely browned on the bottom. Flip the burgers and cook for about 3 more minutes, or until browned on the second side and cooked through.

3. Place 1 patty on the bottom half of each bun and top with the lettuce and tomato. Cover with the top half of each bun. Serve immediately.

Cast-iron tip: When cooking burgers, it's best to place them in the hot skillet and then let them cook undisturbed until they are nicely browned on the bottom. Don't press down on the patties as they cook, or you'll squeeze out the juices that make the burgers delicious.

Chicken and Black Bean Tacos

Serves 4 / **Prep time: 10 minutes** / **Cook time: 15 minutes**

I love whipping up these quick skillet chicken-and-bean tacos. You can fill the tortillas yourself or set them up taco bar–style with lots of toppings to choose from—sour cream, salsa, guacamole, and anything else you like!

8 corn tortillas

1 pound boneless, skinless chicken, cut into bite-size pieces

Juice of 1 lime

1 tablespoon chili powder

½ teaspoon kosher salt

1 tablespoon cooking oil

½ onion, diced

1 garlic clove, minced

1 (15-ounce) can black beans, drained and rinsed

1 (14.5-ounce) can fire-roasted diced tomatoes with their juices

1 cup shredded Cheddar cheese

Shredded lettuce, for garnish (optional)

Salsa, for garnish (optional)

1. Preheat the oven to 400°F.

2. Wrap the tortillas in aluminum foil and heat in the oven while you prepare the chicken and beans.

3. In a medium bowl, combine the chicken, lime juice, chili powder, and salt and toss to mix well.

4. In a skillet over medium-high heat, heat the oil until it shimmers. Add the onion and cook, stirring occasionally, for about 5 minutes, or until softened. Add the garlic and stir for about 20 seconds.

5. Add the chicken and cook, stirring frequently, for about 5 minutes, or until the chicken is cooked through and begins to brown. Add the beans and tomatoes with their juices and cook, stirring occasionally, for 5 minutes, or until the liquid has mostly evaporated and everything is heated through.

6. Fill the warmed tortillas with the chicken-and-bean mixture. Top with the cheese, lettuce (if using), and salsa (if using), and serve immediately.

Variation tip: To make beef tacos instead, use a tender cut like sirloin, cut into bite-size pieces, and cook as you would the chicken.

Crispy Fried Chicken Strips

Serves 4 / Prep time: 10 minutes / Cook time: 20 minutes

A quick fried chicken dinner is a weeknight dream. Kids and adults love this combo, especially if you serve it with an assortment of dipping sauces—ketchup, ranch dressing, barbecue sauce, or whatever you prefer. Be sure to fry the chicken until the pieces are a dark golden brown and satisfyingly crispy.

Cooking oil, for frying

1½ cups all-purpose flour

1½ teaspoons kosher salt, divided

1 teaspoon freshly ground black pepper, divided

1 large egg, beaten

2 tablespoons water

1½ pounds chicken tenders

1. Fill a skillet with about 2 inches of oil and heat it over medium-high heat until it shimmers.

2. While the oil is heating, in a large bowl, stir together the flour, ¾ teaspoon of salt, and ½ teaspoon of pepper.

3. In a second bowl, whisk the egg with the water.

4. Season the chicken with the remaining ¾ teaspoon of salt and ½ teaspoon of pepper. Dredge the chicken pieces first in the flour, then in the egg, and then once again in the flour.

5. When the oil is hot, drop the chicken pieces in, about 5 at a time, and cook, turning if needed, for about 8 minutes per batch, or until dark golden brown on all sides. Transfer the cooked chicken pieces to a paper towel–lined plate. Serve hot.

Cast-iron tip: Using a smaller skillet means that you can use less oil, but you'll need to cook more batches because you don't want to crowd the pan. I like to use a 12-inch skillet for this recipe, and I fill it with enough oil to come halfway up the sides of the chicken pieces so that they can brown on one side completely and then the other.

Spicy Chicken Meatballs with Fresh Basil over Noodles

Serves 4 / **Prep time: 10 minutes** / **Cook time: 15 minutes**

My son would be happy to eat classic spaghetti and meatballs every single night, but I prefer to change up the flavors now and then. This noodle-and-meatballs dinner departs from the traditional dish by using ground chicken instead of beef or lamb and adding hot peppers to the mix. Fresh basil elevates the flavors. You can use any type of noodles you like here, from Thai-style rice noodles to classic Italian spaghetti.

1 pound ground chicken

¾ cup panko bread crumbs

1 large egg

1 shallot, finely minced

3 garlic cloves, minced

1 or 2 red serrano peppers, seeded and minced

4 tablespoons chopped fresh basil, divided

1 teaspoon kosher salt

½ teaspoon freshly ground black pepper

1 tablespoon soy sauce

12 ounces dried noodles

3 tablespoons extra-virgin olive oil, divided

1. In a medium bowl, combine the chicken, bread crumbs, egg, shallot, garlic, serrano peppers, 2 tablespoons of basil, salt, pepper, and soy sauce. Mix well, then form the mixture into 1½-inch balls.

2. Cook the noodles according to the package directions.

3. While the noodles cook, in a skillet over medium-high heat, heat 2 tablespoons of oil. Add the meatballs and cook in a single layer, turning occasionally, for about 12 minutes, or until browned on all sides and cooked through.

4. Drain, transfer to a serving bowl, and toss with the remaining 1 tablespoon of oil and the remaining 2 tablespoons of basil.

5. Toss the cooked noodles with the meatballs and serve immediately.

Variation tip: You can substitute any ground meat you like for the chicken—turkey, pork, beef, or even lamb.

Chicken and Rice with Warm Spices

Serves 4 / **Prep time: 5 minutes** / **Cook time: 20 minutes**

A spice mixture commonly used in Lebanese cooking, *bahārāt* is a combination of black pepper, coriander, cumin, paprika, allspice, cardamom, cinnamon, cloves, and nutmeg. Because you probably won't find bahārāt in your regular supermarket, this recipe uses a pumpkin pie spice seasoning mix, which contains five of the spices in bahārāt—allspice, cardamom, cinnamon, cloves, and nutmeg.

1 teaspoon kosher salt, plus a pinch

½ teaspoon freshly ground black pepper, plus a pinch

1 teaspoon ground cumin

1 teaspoon pumpkin pie spice

4 boneless, skinless chicken breasts, or 6 boneless, skinless chicken thighs

3 tablespoons extra-virgin olive oil, divided

1¼ cups uncooked long-grain white rice

3 cups chicken broth

1. In a small bowl, stir together 1 teaspoon of salt, ½ teaspoon of pepper, the cumin, and the pumpkin pie spice.

2. Put the chicken in a medium bowl and toss it with 2 tablespoons of oil. Season the chicken with half of the seasoning mixture.

3. In a skillet over medium-high heat, heat the remaining 1 tablespoon of oil until it shimmers. Add the chicken and cook, turning it over once, for 2 to 3 minutes per side, or until browned on both sides. Transfer the chicken to a plate.

4. Add the rice, broth, remaining pinch of salt, remaining pinch of pepper, and remaining half of the seasoning mixture to the skillet and stir to mix well. Add the browned chicken to the skillet, laying it on top of the rice. Cover the skillet with a lid or aluminum foil and cook for about 15 minutes, or until the rice has absorbed the liquid and is tender and the chicken is cooked through. Serve hot.

Pan-Seared Chicken with Brussels Sprouts, Bacon, and Apples

Serves 4 / Prep time: **5 minutes** / Cook time: **25 minutes**

I love to combine Brussels sprouts with sweet, tender apples because the sweetness of the fruit balances the slight bitterness of the vegetable. Bacon adds depth of flavor and a hint of smoke. This chicken dish is simple and quick to make but feels like a real old-fashioned meal for company.

4 thick-cut bacon slices

4 to 6 boneless, skin-on chicken thighs

1 teaspoon kosher salt

½ teaspoon freshly ground black pepper

1 pound Brussels sprouts, shredded

1 large Fuji or Granny Smith apple, peeled, cored, and cubed

½ cup dry white wine

1. Preheat the oven to 425°F.

2. Heat a skillet over medium heat. Add the bacon and cook for about 6 minutes, or until cooked through. Remove the bacon, transferring it to a paper towel–lined plate, leaving the bacon fat behind. Crumble or chop the bacon.

3. Season the chicken with the salt and pepper. Raise the heat under the skillet to medium-high and add the chicken, skin-side down. Cook for about 5 minutes, or until nicely browned on both sides. Transfer the chicken to a plate.

4. Add the Brussels sprouts and apple to the skillet and cook, stirring occasionally, for 2 minutes. Add the wine and cook, stirring, for about 2 minutes, or until reduced by half. Return the bacon to the pan and then add the chicken, arranging the pieces in a single layer. Spoon the sauce, Brussels sprouts, bacon, and apples over the chicken pieces.

5. Transfer the skillet to the oven and cook for about 10 more minutes, or until the chicken is cooked through and the Brussels sprouts are tender.

Prosciutto-Wrapped Chicken Breast Fillets

Serves **4** / Prep time: **10 minutes** / Cook time: **20 minutes**

Chicken breast on its own can be hard to get right—it often dries out during cooking. Cutting the breasts into thin cutlets and then wrapping them in prosciutto before cooking helps keep them moist.

2 boneless, skinless chicken breasts, halved horizontally to form 4 fillets or cutlets

1 teaspoon salt

½ teaspoon freshly ground black pepper

4 slices prosciutto

2 tablespoons olive oil

1 shallot, minced

1 teaspoon all-purpose flour

⅓ cup dry white wine

½ cup chicken broth

2 tablespoons unsalted butter

1. Season the chicken fillets with the salt and pepper on both sides, then wrap 1 slice of prosciutto around each chicken fillet.

2. In a skillet over medium heat, heat the oil until it shimmers. Add the prosciutto-wrapped chicken to the skillet and cook for about 5 minutes, or until browned on the bottom. Flip over and cook for about 3 more minutes, or until the chicken is cooked through. Transfer the chicken to a serving platter and tent with aluminum foil.

3. Add the shallot to the skillet and cook, stirring frequently, for about 3 minutes, or until softened. Sprinkle with flour and cook, stirring, for 1 minute.

4. Add the wine and cook, stirring and scraping up the browned bits, for about 2 minutes, or until the liquid reduces by half. Add the broth and continue to cook, stirring frequently, for 4 more minutes, or until the liquid again reduces by about half.

5. Adjust the heat to low and add the butter to the skillet, stirring until it is fully incorporated.

6. Return the chicken to the skillet and simmer for about 1 minute, or until heated through.

7. Serve hot with the sauce drizzled over the top.

Spiced Chicken Stew with Almonds

Serves 4 / **Prep time: 5 minutes** / **Cook time: 25 minutes**

This savory chicken stew gets its flavor from the spice mixture garam masala and sweet raisins. This stew makes a satisfying meal served over couscous to soak up the saucy goodness.

2 tablespoons sliced almonds

1 tablespoon extra-virgin olive oil

1½ pounds boneless, skinless chicken thighs

1½ teaspoons kosher salt, divided

¾ teaspoon freshly ground black pepper, divided

1 onion, thinly sliced

2 carrots, cut into thin coins

1 garlic clove, minced

2 teaspoons garam masala

1 cup chicken broth

½ cup raisins

Juice of ½ lemon

1. Heat a skillet over medium-high heat. Add the almonds and cook, shaking the pan frequently, for 2 to 3 minutes, or until fragrant and beginning to turn golden brown. Transfer to a bowl.

2. Add the oil to the skillet and heat until it shimmers. Season the chicken with ½ teaspoon of salt and ¼ teaspoon of pepper and add it to the skillet. Cook for about 3 minutes, or until the bottom is nicely browned. Flip the chicken and cook for 3 more minutes, or until the second side browns. Transfer to a plate.

3. Add the onion to the skillet, and cook, stirring frequently, for about 3 minutes, or until softened. Add the carrots and cook, stirring occasionally, for about 5 minutes, or until they begin to soften. Stir in the garlic, garam masala, remaining 1 teaspoon of salt, and remaining ½ teaspoon of pepper and cook for 30 seconds. Stir in the broth and raisins.

4. Return the chicken to the skillet, adjust the heat to low, and simmer, uncovered, for about 10 minutes, or until cooked through.

5. Squeeze the lemon juice over the chicken and serve garnished with the toasted almonds.

Chicken Chile Verde

Serves 4 / **Prep time: 10 minutes** / **Cook time: 20 minutes**

Tart tomatillos and roasted green chilies give this quick chile verde layers of tangy and smoky flavor. Serve it topped with your choice of crunchy tortilla chips, shredded cheese, diced avocado, guacamole, sour cream, hot sauce or salsa, and diced onions.

2 tablespoons cooking oil

1 pound boneless, skinless chicken thighs, cut into bite-size pieces

1½ teaspoons kosher salt, divided

¾ teaspoon freshly ground black pepper, divided

1 onion, diced

1 (14.5-ounce) can diced tomatoes with their juices

1 cup chopped fresh tomatillos (about 6 tomatillos, papery skin removed)

1 (4-ounce) can diced green chilies with their juices

2 garlic cloves, minced

¾ teaspoon ground cumin

½ teaspoon dried oregano

1. In a skillet over medium-high heat, heat the oil until it shimmers. Season the chicken with ½ teaspoon of salt and ¼ teaspoon of pepper. Add the chicken to the skillet and cook, stirring occasionally, for about 5 minutes, or until opaque but not cooked through. Transfer the chicken to a bowl or plate.

2. Add the onion to the skillet and cook, stirring occasionally, for about 3 minutes, or until softened. Add the tomatoes and their juices, tomatillos, green chilies, garlic, cumin, oregano, and the remaining 1 teaspoon of salt and ½ teaspoon of pepper. Bring to a simmer, then reduce the heat to medium-low and simmer for about 10 minutes, or until most of the liquid has evaporated. Return the cooked chicken to the skillet and cook for about 2 more minutes, or until heated through. Serve hot.

Make it easier: If you don't want to bother with fresh tomatillos, use 1 (12-ounce) can of whole tomatillos, drained and diced.

Stir-Fried Ground Chicken with Chiles and Basil

Serves 4 / **Prep time: 10 minutes** / **Cook time: 15 minutes**

This quick stir-fried dish is one of my go-to weeknight recipes. It's light, healthy, and, of course, quick to make. What I love most about it, though, is that it is full of the simple, fresh flavors of basil and chiles.

2 tablespoons cooking oil

1 small onion, thinly sliced

2 garlic cloves, minced

1 pound ground chicken

2 jalapeño or serrano peppers, seeded and diced (leave the seeds in for more heat)

1 tablespoon fish sauce

1 tablespoon brown sugar

Juice of 1 lime

½ cup julienned fresh basil

1. In a skillet over medium-high heat, heat the oil until it shimmers. Add the onion and garlic and cook, stirring occasionally, for about 5 minutes, or until softened.

2. Add the chicken and cook, stirring and breaking up the meat with a spatula, for about 5 minutes, or until the meat is cooked through and beginning to brown.

3. Add the jalapeños, fish sauce, and brown sugar and cook, stirring to mix well, for 1 to 2 more minutes.

4. Just before serving, stir in the lime juice and basil.

Sesame-Ginger Chicken

Serves 4 / **Prep time:** **10 minutes, plus 10 minutes to marinate** / **Cook time:** **10 minutes**

Tender chicken is a perfect partner for ginger's fresh bite. Oyster sauce is a sweet-savory sauce used in Chinese cooking. It is made from oysters, sugar, and salt or soy sauce and is sold in most supermarkets.

3 tablespoons soy sauce, divided

2 tablespoons oyster sauce, divided

1 teaspoon sesame oil, plus 1 tablespoon

3 teaspoons sugar, divided

1½ pounds boneless, skinless chicken, cut into bite-size pieces

2 garlic cloves, minced

2 teaspoons minced peeled fresh ginger

2 green bell peppers, thinly sliced

2 cups chicken broth

2 tablespoons cornstarch whisked with 2 tablespoons cold water

2 tablespoons toasted sesame seeds

1. In a large bowl, whisk 2 tablespoons of soy sauce, 1 tablespoon of oyster sauce, 1 teaspoon of sesame oil, and 1 teaspoon of sugar. Toss in the chicken to coat. Let marinate for 10 minutes.

2. In a skillet over medium-high heat, heat the remaining 1 tablespoon of sesame oil. Add the garlic and ginger. Cook, stirring, for about 30 seconds.

3. Add the marinated chicken, discarding the marinade, and cook, stirring occasionally, for about 3 minutes, or until browned and just cooked through. Transfer the chicken to a plate.

4. Add the bell peppers to the skillet and cook, stirring, for about 5 minutes, or until softened.

5. Return the chicken to the skillet and add the broth, the remaining 1 tablespoon of soy sauce, the remaining 1 tablespoon of oyster sauce, and the remaining 2 teaspoons of sugar. Bring to a boil, then add the cornstarch mixture and cook, stirring, for about 2 minutes, or until the sauce thickens. Serve hot, garnished with the sesame seeds.

Variation tip: If you don't like bell peppers, use thinly sliced carrots or broccoli florets.

MEAT

Pan-Seared Rib-Eye Steaks with Gorgonzola Butter, page 111

Stir-Fried Mango Beef

Serves 4 / Prep time: **10 minutes** / Cook time: **15 minutes**

There was a great Californian Chinese restaurant I used to visit often, and one of my favorite dishes there was mango beef. The sweet mango and savory steak balance each other beautifully. The savory sauce starts with soy sauce and mirin (a sweet rice wine for cooking) and is studded with garlic and ginger. I love spicy food and usually add a hearty spoonful of hot chili paste to counter the fruit's sweetness. Serve this saucy dish over rice.

¼ cup soy sauce

1 tablespoon mirin

1 teaspoon brown sugar

1 pound flank steak, cut into thin strips

1 tablespoon cooking oil

2 garlic cloves, minced

1 tablespoon minced peeled fresh ginger

3 cups broccoli florets

1 mango, peeled, pitted, and cubed

1 tablespoon cornstarch mixed with 1 tablespoon water

1. In a large bowl, whisk together the soy sauce, mirin, and brown sugar. Add the steak and toss to coat.

2. In a skillet over medium-high heat, heat the oil. Add the meat, reserving the marinade, and cook, stirring frequently, for about 4 minutes, or until the steak browns on both sides. Stir in the garlic and ginger and then add the broccoli. Cook, stirring frequently, for about 5 more minutes, or until the broccoli is tender. Add the mango and the reserved marinade to the skillet and bring to a boil. Add the cornstarch slurry and cook, stirring, for 1 to 2 minutes more, or until the sauce thickens. Serve immediately.

Variation tip: Mirin is a sweet rice wine for cooking. If you don't have it, you can substitute white wine or sherry, or simply leave it out.

Beef and Sweet Potatoes in Thai Curry Sauce with Coconut Milk

Serves 4 / **Prep time: 10 minutes** / **Cook time: 20 minutes**

This dish is so easy and so tasty that you may never order take-out again. The sauce has a rich coconut milk base seasoned with Thai curry paste. You can find Thai curry paste in most supermarkets or in Asian groceries. This single ingredient carries many layers of flavor. Don't skip the fresh basil at the end, as the herby flavor really ties the dish together.

2 tablespoons cooking oil

1 (15-ounce) can unsweetened coconut milk, divided

1 to 3 tablespoons Thai red curry paste

Grated zest of 1 lime

1 large sweet potato, peeled and diced

1 large onion, thinly sliced

1½ pounds flank steak, cut into thin strips

1 large red bell pepper, seeded and cut into strips

Juice of 1 lime

1 tablespoon fish sauce

¼ cup chopped fresh basil

1. In a skillet over medium-high heat, heat the oil. Add ½ cup of coconut milk, the curry paste to taste, and the lime zest and cook, stirring occasionally, for about 3 minutes, or until the mixture bubbles and thickens.

2. Add the remaining coconut milk, sweet potato, and onion and bring to a boil. Cook, stirring occasionally, for about 10 minutes, or until the sweet potato is tender.

3. Reduce the heat to medium-low and stir in the steak, bell pepper, lime juice, and fish sauce. Simmer for 6 to 8 minutes, or until the sauce is thick and the meat is fully cooked. Just before serving, stir in the basil. Serve hot.

Variation tip: Thai curry paste varies widely in its spice level from brand to brand. Start with 1 tablespoon and add more as needed to get the amount of flavor and heat you like. You can add more curry paste in step 3.

Seared Flank Steak Salad with Warm Balsamic-Bacon Vinaigrette

Serves 4 / Prep time: **10 minutes** / Cook time: **15 minutes**

I'm a fan of having a big salad as a meal, and this one has everything I love—perfectly seared flank steak, smoky bacon, tender baby spinach, and a sweet balsamic vinaigrette. A cast-iron skillet works magic on steak, and for this recipe, it's also used to crisp the bacon and make the warm balsamic dressing.

1 pound flank steak

¾ teaspoon kosher salt

½ teaspoon freshly ground black pepper

6 bacon slices, diced

1 small red onion, diced

2 tablespoons chopped sundried tomatoes in oil, drained

¼ cup balsamic vinegar

1 teaspoon sugar

1 teaspoon Dijon mustard

6 cups baby spinach leaves (1 [5-ounce] package)

1. Season the steak on both sides with the salt and pepper.

2. In a skillet over medium-high heat, cook the bacon, stirring occasionally, for about 5 minutes, or until crisp. Transfer the bacon to a paper towel–lined plate. Leave the fat in the pan.

3. Add the steak to the skillet and cook for about 3 minutes per side, or until nicely browned. Remove from skillet and let rest for 5 minutes.

4. Lower the heat to medium and add the onion and sundried tomatoes to the skillet. Cook, stirring, for about 3 minutes, or just until the onion is softened. Add the vinegar, sugar, and mustard and cook, stirring, for 1 more minute. Remove the skillet from the heat.

5. In a large bowl, toss together the spinach and about half of the warm vinaigrette.

6. Once the steak has rested, cut it against the grain into ¼-inch-thick slices.

7. Divide the spinach among 4 serving plates, top each with one-quarter of the sliced steak, sprinkle the bacon over the salads, and drizzle the remaining vinaigrette over the top. Serve immediately.

Cast-iron tip: Cooking the bacon in the skillet first adds to your fantastic coat of seasoning and also means that you don't need to add any oil before cooking the steak. You'll get all that great bacon flavor, too.

Hoisin Beef

Serves 4 / Prep time: 5 minutes / Cook time: 15 minutes

Hoisin sauce is a thick, brown sauce with sweet and savory flavors including from fermented soybeans or soy sauce, sugar, sesame seeds, vinegar, and garlic. Teriyaki sauce is made from soy sauce, rice wine, ginger, and sugar. Combining the two sauces makes a quick but complexly flavored marinade for a beef dish that only requires five ingredients. This stir-fry with snow peas can be on the table in the time it takes to cook a pot of rice to serve with it.

¼ cup teriyaki sauce

3 tablespoons hoisin sauce

1 pound flank steak, thinly sliced against the grain

2 tablespoons cooking oil

1 pound snow peas, halved

1. In a large bowl, whisk together the teriyaki sauce and hoisin sauce. Add the steak and toss to coat.

2. In a skillet over medium-high heat, heat the oil until it shimmers. Add the steak, reserving the marinade, and cook, stirring occasionally, for about 5 minutes, or until the meat is browned and just cooked through. Transfer the meat to a plate.

3. Add the snow peas to the skillet and cook, stirring frequently, for about 3 minutes, or until tender.

4. Return the steak to the pan along with the reserved marinade. Bring to a boil, reduce the heat to medium, and simmer for 3 to 4 minutes, or until the sauce thickens slightly. Serve immediately.

Variation tip: You can use ground beef, turkey, chicken, or pork in place of the flank steak here. Brown the ground meat in the skillet first, remove it, and then cook the snow peas. Return the meat to the skillet with the teriyaki and hoisin sauces and cook until the sauce thickens.

Beef Taco Skillet

Serves 4 / **Prep time: 10 minutes** / **Cook time: 15 minutes**

Just about everyone loves tacos, but sometimes even that simple dish seems like too much trouble. This all-in-one skillet version of your favorite ground beef tacos is the answer. It has all the taco flavors you love, but it's all cooked together in a single skillet. Perfection!

1 pound ground beef

1 onion, diced

1 red bell pepper, seeded and diced

2 garlic cloves, diced

2 tablespoons chili powder

1 teaspoon kosher salt

½ teaspoon freshly ground black pepper

1½ cups frozen corn kernels

10 (6-inch) corn tortillas, cut into 1½-inch strips

1 cup mild or medium salsa

1¼ cups shredded sharp Cheddar cheese, divided

1. Heat a skillet over medium-high heat. Add the beef and cook, stirring occasionally, for about 5 minutes, or until browned. Drain off the excess fat.

2. Add the onion, bell pepper, garlic, chili powder, salt, and pepper and cook, stirring, for about 5 minutes, or until the vegetables are softened.

3. Stir in the corn, tortilla strips, salsa, and 1 cup of cheese and cook, stirring occasionally, for about 5 minutes, or until heated through.

4. Remove the skillet from the heat, sprinkle the remaining ¼ cup of cheese over the top, and let stand until the cheese is melted. Serve hot.

Cast-iron tip: Because cast-iron skillets are oven-safe, you can stick the cheese-topped dish under the broiler to melt the cheese more quickly, if you like.

BLT Pasta Bake

Serves **4** / Prep time: **5 minutes** / Cook time: **25 minutes**

Okay, we've substituted spinach for the lettuce, so it's really a BST, but the result is the same: delicious. Salty bacon combines with sweet tomatoes and fresh greens to create a pasta dish that has it all.

8 ounces fusilli, penne, or other short pasta

4 bacon slices

3 garlic cloves, thinly sliced

1 (28-ounce) can crushed tomatoes

¼ teaspoon red pepper flakes

4 cups chopped spinach leaves or other leafy greens

½ teaspoon kosher salt

½ cup part-skim ricotta cheese

¼ cup freshly grated Parmesan cheese

1 cup shredded mozzarella cheese

1. Preheat the oven to 450°F.

2. Bring a large pot of salted water to a boil. Cook the pasta according to the package directions. Drain, reserving ½ cup of the pasta water.

3. While the pasta is cooking, in a skillet over medium heat, cook the bacon, flipping once, for about 5 minutes, or until crisp and brown. Drain it on a paper towel–lined plate, then crumble it.

4. Pour off most of the bacon fat from the skillet and return it to the stovetop over medium heat. Add the garlic and cook, stirring, for 30 seconds. Add the tomatoes, reserved pasta water, red pepper flakes, spinach, and salt. Bring to a simmer over medium-high heat and cook for about 5 minutes, or until the sauce bubbles and begins to thicken and the spinach wilts.

5. In a small bowl, stir together the ricotta and Parmesan.

6. Stir the cooked pasta and mozzarella into the sauce. Dollop the ricotta-and-Parmesan mixture on top, then sprinkle the bacon over the cheese. Bake for about 10 minutes, or until the whole thing is bubbling and the cheese is melted. Serve hot.

Steak Fajitas

Serves 4 / Prep time: **5 minutes, plus 10 minutes to marinate** / Cook time: **15 minutes**

Fajitas make an ideal one-skillet meal. A quick stir-fry of seasoned meat and veggies is a perfect filling for warm flour tortillas. Serve these as is, or add your favorite salsa, guacamole, sour cream, or other toppings.

3 tablespoons extra-virgin olive oil, divided

Juice of 1 lime

2 garlic cloves, minced

1 tablespoon chili powder

1 teaspoon dried oregano

1 teaspoon ground cumin

1 teaspoon kosher salt, plus a pinch

1 teaspoon freshly ground black pepper, plus a pinch

1 pound flank steak or top sirloin, thinly sliced against the grain

8 flour tortillas

2 bell peppers (any color or a combination), thinly sliced

1 onion, thinly sliced

1. Preheat the oven to 350°F.

2. In a large bowl, combine 1 tablespoon of oil, the lime juice, garlic, chili powder, oregano, cumin, 1 teaspoon of salt, and 1 teaspoon of pepper. Add the steak and toss to coat well. Marinate for 10 minutes.

3. Wrap the tortillas in aluminum foil and place them in the oven to heat for 10 minutes.

4. While the tortillas warm, in a skillet over high heat, heat 1 tablespoon of oil until it begins to shimmer. Add the bell peppers, onion, remaining pinch of salt, and remaining pinch of pepper. Cook, stirring occasionally, for about 5 minutes, or until the vegetables are softened. Transfer the vegetables to a plate.

5. Add the remaining 1 tablespoon of oil to the skillet and heat over medium-high heat. Add the steak, discarding the marinade, and cook, stirring frequently, for about 5 minutes, or until browned and just cooked through. Return the vegetables to the skillet and cook, stirring, for about 2 minutes, or until heated through. Serve immediately with the warm tortillas for wrapping.

Stir-Fried Rice Noodles with Pork and Shrimp

Serves 4 / Prep time: **10 minutes** / Cook time: **15 minutes**

I love using Thai or Vietnamese rice noodles for skillet cooking. All you have to do is soak the noodles in hot water until they soften, and then you can quickly stir-fry them in the skillet. Rice noodles have a great chewy texture that is quite different from wheat noodles. In this dish, the noodles are studded with savory pork, plump shrimp, and golden egg.

1 (10-ounce) package dried rice stick noodles

2 tablespoons soy sauce

2 teaspoons toasted sesame oil

½ teaspoon sugar

4 garlic cloves, minced

4 tablespoons cooking oil, divided

2 large eggs, beaten with ⅛ teaspoon kosher salt

½ cup sliced onion

8 ounces peeled and deveined medium shrimp

8 ounces diced roast pork or ham

1. Soak the rice noodles according to the package directions, then drain.

2. In a small bowl, stir together the soy sauce, sesame oil, sugar, and garlic.

3. In a skillet over high heat, heat 1 tablespoon of oil. Add the eggs and cook, stirring, for about 2 minutes, or until set. Transfer the eggs to a large bowl and chop into pieces using a spatula.

4. Add 1 tablespoon of oil to the skillet. Add the onion and cook, stirring occasionally, for about 5 minutes, or until tender and beginning to brown.

5. Add 1 tablespoon of oil and then add the shrimp. Cook, turning occasionally, for about 2 minutes, or until the shrimp are just cooked through. Add the roast pork and cook, stirring occasionally, for about 2 more minutes, or until heated through. Transfer the meat and veggies to the bowl with the eggs.

6. Add the remaining 1 tablespoon of oil to the skillet, then add the softened noodles. Cook, tossing, for about 3 minutes, or until the noodles begin to brown. Add the sauce mixture and cook, tossing to coat the noodles with the sauce. Return the meat and vegetables to the skillet and toss to combine. Serve hot.

Variation tip: You can add 2 sliced heads of bok choy for a bit of green. Add it along with the onion in step 4.

Pork Banh Mi Sandwiches

Serves 4 / **Prep time: 15 minutes** / **Cook time: 10 minutes**

These quick banh mi sandwiches are filled with caramelized strips of pork, jalapeño peppers, quick pickled carrots and daikon radish, and cilantro. The sandwich is the perfect combo of crusty bread, creamy mayo, spicy peppers, crisp-tangy pickled vegetables, and fresh herbs.

¼ cup fish sauce

4 tablespoons sugar, divided

2 garlic cloves, minced

1¼ pounds pork tenderloin, cut into 2-inch strips

½ cup white vinegar

½ cup water

½ teaspoon kosher salt

1 carrot, shredded

½ daikon radish, shredded

2 tablespoons vegetable oil

4 tablespoons mayonnaise

4 French rolls, split

2 jalapeño peppers, thinly sliced

8 cilantro sprigs

1. In a medium bowl, combine the fish sauce, 2 tablespoons of sugar, and garlic. Add the pork and toss to coat. Let marinate while you prep the other ingredients.

2. To make the quick pickled carrots, combine the vinegar, water, salt, and remaining 2 tablespoons of sugar in a saucepan. Heat over medium-high heat until the sugar dissolves. Remove from the heat and add the carrot and radish, cover the pan, and let stand for about 10 minutes while you cook the pork.

3. In a skillet over high heat, heat the oil. Add the marinated pork, discarding the marinade, and cook for 2 to 3 minutes per side, or until nicely browned on both sides.

4. To assemble the sandwiches, spread 1 tablespoon of mayonnaise on one cut side of each of the rolls. Add the cooked pork, pickled radish and carrots, jalapeños, and cilantro. Serve immediately.

Variation tip: If you don't have daikon radish, use regular radishes and slice them thinly.

Cheddar-Stuffed Burgers

Serves 4 / **Prep time: 10 minutes** / **Cook time: 10 minutes**

A cast-iron skillet gives a meaty burger the perfect sear. To ensure that your burgers are juicy and flavorful, don't overwork the meat as you mix it and form the patties. And resist the urge to push down on the burgers as they cook, which presses those delicious juices out where they turn into steam and evaporate. Keep all that goodness inside! Serve the burgers with whatever condiments you like.

1 pound ground beef

1 tablespoon Dijon mustard

½ teaspoon kosher salt

½ teaspoon freshly ground black pepper

8 tablespoons shredded Cheddar cheese

4 hamburger buns

1 large tomato, thinly sliced

4 lettuce leaves

1. In a medium bowl, mix together the beef, mustard, salt, and pepper. Using your hands, form the mixture into 8 thin patties. Place 2 tablespoons of shredded cheese on top of each of 4 burger patties. Top with the remaining patties and press the edges together to seal them well so that you have 4 burgers with cheese inside.

2. Heat a skillet over medium-high heat. Add the burgers and cook for about 5 minutes, or until nicely browned on the bottom. Flip the burgers over and cook for 4 to 5 more minutes, or until the second sides are browned.

3. If desired, lightly toast the buns.

4. Place the burgers on the bottom halves of the buns, then top each with a tomato slice, a lettuce leaf, and the bun top. Serve immediately, with your desired condiments.

Variation tip: You can use any type of cheese you like here. I love to substitute a blue cheese like Gorgonzola or a creamy cheese like Brie.

Pan-Seared Pork Chops with Cabbage

Serves **4** / Prep time: **5 minutes** / Cook time: **15 minutes**

These pork chops are seasoned with a spicy Caribbean spice mixture and quickly seared in the skillet. While the pork chops rest, the cabbage is cooked in the same skillet, picking up the spicy flavors of the jerk seasoning and making this a perfectly timed meal.

½ teaspoon kosher salt, plus more as needed

¼ teaspoon freshly ground black pepper, plus more as needed

2 tablespoons Caribbean jerk seasoning

1/2 teaspoon red pepper flakes

½ teaspoon onion powder

4 thick-cut boneless pork chops, butterflied

1 tablespoon cooking oil

2 tablespoons unsalted butter

½ head cabbage, thinly sliced

1. In a small bowl, mix together the salt, black pepper, jerk seasoning, red pepper flakes, and onion powder. Rub the seasoning mixture all over the pork chops.

2. In a skillet over medium-high heat, heat the oil. Add the seasoned pork chops and cook for 3 to 5 minutes, or until golden brown on the bottom. Flip the chops over and cook on other side for 3 to 5 more minutes, or until browned on the second side and cooked through. Transfer the pork chops to a plate and tent them with aluminum foil. Let the meat rest while you cook the cabbage.

3. In the skillet, melt the butter over medium heat. Add the cabbage and cook, stirring, for about 4 minutes, or until nice and tender. Taste and add more salt and pepper as needed.

4. Serve the pork chops and cabbage together.

Cast-iron tip: Cast iron is a great cooking surface for meat because it quickly sears the outside, sealing in the flavorful juices. To let those juices redistribute throughout the meat, always let the meat rest for at least 5 minutes before serving.

Pan-Seared Rib-Eye Steaks with Gorgonzola Butter

Serves 4 / Prep time: **5 minutes** / Cook time: **10 minutes**

Cast-iron pans and thick, juicy steaks are a match made in heaven. The high heat of the skillet is ideal for getting a good sear on the meat to seal in all the flavorful juices. And the rich, flavorful Gorgonzola butter is a truly decadent finishing touch.

¼ cup crumbled Gorgonzola cheese, at room temperature

4 tablespoons (½ stick) unsalted butter, at room temperature

4 rib-eye steaks, at room temperature

1 teaspoon kosher salt

½ teaspoon freshly ground black pepper

1 tablespoon olive oil

1 tablespoon chopped fresh parsley

1. In a small bowl, stir together the Gorgonzola and butter until well blended. Refrigerate until ready to serve.

2. Season both sides of each steak generously with the salt and pepper.

3. Heat a skillet over medium heat. Add the oil, swirling the pan to coat well. Place the steaks in the skillet and cook for 2 minutes, or until the bottom browns. Flip the steaks over and cook for 2 minutes on the second side. This will cook the steaks to about medium-rare. If you prefer a well-done steak, add 1 or 2 minutes to the cooking time on each side.

4. Remove the skillet from the heat and tent loosely with aluminum foil. Let the steaks rest in the skillet for 5 minutes.

5. Serve the steaks with a dollop of the Gorgonzola butter on top and a sprinkling of the parsley.

Cast-iron tip: Depending on the size of your skillet, you may need to cook the steaks in batches. If so, remove the first batch to a plate and tent loosely with foil while cooking the second batch. Transfer the first batch to serving plates when you pull the second batch out of the skillet to rest.

Bolognese Pasta Sauce

Serves 4 / Prep time: **5 minutes** / Cook time: **25 minutes**

To make a good Bolognese sauce, you have to layer the ingredients for deep, rich flavor. This quick version combines pancetta and Italian sausage for intense flavor in just 30 minutes. Serve over cooked spaghetti, topped with grated Parmesan cheese if you tolerate dairy.

4 ounces diced pancetta or bacon

1 onion, finely diced

1 pound Italian sausage (hot or mild)

3 garlic cloves, minced

1 cup red wine

1 (28-ounce) can crushed tomatoes

¼ cup tomato paste

2 teaspoons dried oregano

1 teaspoon kosher salt

½ teaspoon red pepper flakes

1. Heat a skillet over medium-high heat. Add the pancetta and onion, and cook, stirring frequently, for about 5 minutes, or until the onion is soft and translucent. Add the sausage and garlic and cook, stirring and breaking up the meat with a spatula, for 6 to 8 minutes, or until browned.

2. Stir in the wine and cook, stirring occasionally, for about 2 minutes, or until most of the liquid has evaporated.

3. Add the tomatoes, tomato paste, oregano, salt, and red pepper flakes and stir to combine. Bring to a simmer and cook over medium heat, stirring occasionally, for 10 minutes, or until the tomatoes break down and the sauce thickens.

Variation tip: You can substitute ground beef, ground pork, or a combination of the two for the Italian sausage.

CHAPTER 8

SNACKS AND SWEETS

Giant Chocolate Chip Cookie, page 123

Skillet Nachos with Chorizo and Homemade Pico de Gallo

Serves 4 / Prep time: **5 minutes** / Cook time: **15 minutes**

Sometimes you just need nachos for dinner. I love using chorizo here because it is full of spices, which means you can use just a few other ingredients and end up with a super flavorful dish. Fresh salsa takes these nachos up a level, and you can always add your favorite toppings!

1 pound Mexican chorizo, casings removed

1 (14-ounce) can refried beans

8 cups corn tortilla chips

2 to 3 cups shredded sharp Cheddar cheese

2 or 3 medium tomatoes, diced

1 large jalapeño pepper, minced (seeded if you prefer less heat)

½ small onion, diced

2 tablespoons chopped fresh cilantro

Juice of 1 lime

¼ to ½ teaspoon kosher salt

½ cup sour cream

1. Preheat the oven to 350°F.

2. Heat a 12-inch skillet over medium-high heat. Cook the chorizo, stirring and breaking up the meat with a spatula, for about 5 minutes, or until the meat browns. Transfer the chorizo to a plate and drain off three-fourths of the fat from the skillet.

3. Dollop a few tablespoons of refried beans around the bottom of the skillet. Top with about half of the tortilla chips. Dollop more refried beans on top of the chips, using about half the can, and then layer on half of the chorizo and half of the cheese. Top with the remaining chips, beans, chorizo, and cheese.

4. Bake for about 10 minutes, or until the cheese melts and bubbles.

5. While the nachos are baking, in a medium bowl, stir together the tomatoes, jalapeño, onion, cilantro, lime juice, and salt.

6. Remove the skillet from the oven and dollop the sour cream and salsa on top.

Baked Brie with Cherry Tomatoes, Fennel, and Balsamic Vinegar

Serves 4 / **Prep time: 10 minutes** / **Cook time: 15 minutes**

Think of this dish as sort of like a fondue, only easier to make and serve. A round of Brie is topped with sweet and tender cherry tomatoes and fennel that have been tossed in olive oil and balsamic vinegar. The whole thing is baked until the vegetables have softened and begun to break down and the cheese is meltingly delicious.

1 pint cherry tomatoes, halved

1 fennel bulb, thinly sliced

3 garlic cloves, minced

¼ cup extra-virgin olive oil

2 tablespoons balsamic vinegar

Kosher salt

Freshly ground black pepper

1 (8-ounce) round Brie cheese

1 baguette, sliced

1. Preheat the oven to 375°F.

2. In a large bowl, toss together the cherry tomatoes, fennel, garlic, oil, and vinegar. Add salt and pepper to taste.

3. Place the whole Brie round in the center of a skillet. Top with the tomato and fennel mixture.

4. Cover the skillet with an ovenproof lid and bake for 15 to 20 minutes, or until the vegetables are tender and the cheese is very hot and melted.

5. Serve immediately with the baguette slices for scooping.

Pan-Fried Spiced Chickpeas

Serves 4 / **Prep time: 5 minutes** / **Cook time: 15 minutes**

Crunchy, flavorful, and nutritious, these crispy fried chickpeas are a great snack alternative to chips. This recipe uses a spice blend called garam masala, which is a combination of cinnamon, pepper, coriander, cumin, and other spices. You can make this more or less spicy as you see fit by adjusting the amount of cayenne.

1 teaspoon garam masala

1 teaspoon ground coriander

1 teaspoon chili powder

½ teaspoon paprika

¼ teaspoon cayenne pepper

½ teaspoon kosher salt, plus more as needed

6 tablespoons cooking oil

2 (15-ounce) cans chickpeas, drained, rinsed, and patted very dry

1. In a medium bowl, make the spice mixture by stirring together the garam masala, coriander, chili powder, paprika, cayenne, and salt.

2. In a skillet over medium-high heat, heat the oil until it shimmers.

3. Working in batches, cook half of the chickpeas, stirring frequently, for 5 to 8 minutes, or until crisp and golden brown. Use a slotted spoon to transfer the chickpeas from the skillet to a paper towel–lined plate to drain. Repeat with the remaining chickpeas.

4. Once the second batch of chickpeas has been cooked and drained, transfer all of the chickpeas to the spice mixture and toss to coat well. Add salt to taste.

5. Serve immediately or store in an airtight container at room temperature for up to a week.

Make it easier: Instead of frying the chickpeas on the stovetop, you can roast them in the skillet. Preheat the oven to 400°F, toss the chickpeas with about 3 tablespoons of oil, and then spread them in an even layer in the skillet. Roast, stirring occasionally, for 20 to 30 minutes, or until crisp and browned, then combine them with the spice mixture.

Jalapeño Popper Dip

Serves 6 to 8 / **Prep time: 5 minutes** / **Cook time: 15 minutes**

Jalapeño poppers are undeniably delicious but somewhat laborious to make. This dip has all the flavors of your favorite jalapeño poppers, and it's perfect for scooping up with tortilla chips. Best of all, this dip takes just 5 minutes to toss together and pop in the oven.

8 ounces cream cheese, at room temperature

1 cup mayonnaise

1½ cups shredded cheese (use Cheddar, pepper jack, Monterey Jack, or a Mexican-style blend)

¾ cup shredded Parmesan cheese, divided

1 (4-ounce) can diced green chilies, drained

4 jalapeño peppers, diced (seeded and ribbed if you want a milder dip)

1 cup panko bread crumbs

4 tablespoons (½ stick) unsalted butter, melted

Tortilla chips, for serving

1. Preheat the oven to 375°F.

2. In a large bowl, combine the cream cheese and mayonnaise and beat with a handheld mixer for about 2 minutes, or until the mixture is fluffy.

3. Stir in the shredded cheese, ½ cup of Parmesan cheese, diced chilies, and the jalapeños.

4. Spread the mixture into a skillet in an even layer.

5. In a small bowl, stir together the bread crumbs, butter, and remaining ¼ cup of Parmesan cheese. Sprinkle the mixture evenly on top of the mixture in the skillet.

6. Bake for 15 to 20 minutes, or until the dip is bubbling and the topping is golden brown and crisp.

7. Serve hot with tortilla chips for dipping.

Variation tip: Add 6 slices of cooked, crumbled bacon along with the cheeses in step 3.

Green Chile and Cheddar Quesadillas

Serves 4 / **Prep time: 5 minutes** / **Cook time: 20 minutes**

Quesadillas are my go-to quick and satisfying snack. This recipe takes them to another level with sautéed peppers and onions. Try serving these quesadillas with spicy salsa, guacamole, and sour cream for dipping. My son could eat this meal every night for dinner and never get bored.

1 tablespoon cooking oil, plus more for brushing the skillet

2 poblano peppers, seeded and diced

½ small onion, thinly sliced

4 (10-inch) flour tortillas

1 cup shredded sharp Cheddar or pepper jack cheese

¼ cup chopped fresh cilantro

1. In a skillet over medium-high heat, heat the oil. Add the peppers and onion and cook, stirring occasionally, for about 5 minutes, or until softened. Transfer the vegetables to a bowl and wipe out the skillet.

2. Brush the skillet with a little more oil. Add a tortilla and let it heat for about 1 minute before flipping it over and letting it heat for another 30 seconds or so. Remove the tortilla from the skillet and set aside.

3. Add a second tortilla to the skillet. Heat for about 1 minute, flip it over, and then place half of the cheese, half of the peppers and onion, and half of the cilantro in an even layer covering the tortilla. Place the first warmed tortilla on top.

4. Cook for 3 to 4 minutes, or until the bottom tortilla is golden brown and the cheese has begun to melt. Carefully flip the whole thing over and cook on the second side for about 3 more minutes, or until the quesadilla is golden brown and the cheese is melted. Remove the quesadilla from the skillet and repeat the process with the remaining ingredients, adding a bit more oil to the skillet if needed.

5. To serve, cut each quesadilla into 8 wedges and serve 4 wedges per person.

Variation tip: I use a robust extra-sharp white Cheddar because I love the flavor, but you can substitute a regular sharp or mild Cheddar, a Mexican cheese blend, or pepper jack if you prefer.

Skillet S'mores Dip

Serves **6 to 8** / Prep time: **5 minutes** / Cook time: **10 minutes**

Have you ever wished you could have all the fun and deliciousness of campfire s'mores without having to build a campfire? This dip is the answer to your dreams. Melted milk chocolate chips are topped with marshmallows that are broiled until toasty and golden brown. Use graham crackers to scoop it up, and you have all the elements of your favorite summer treat without any of the hassle.

1 (12-ounce) package milk chocolate chips

½ cup milk

1 (12-ounce) package marshmallows, halved

1 (14-ounce) package graham crackers

1. Preheat the broiler to high.

2. In a medium microwave-safe bowl, combine the chocolate chips and milk. Heat in 30-second intervals on 50 percent power, stirring in between, until the chocolate is melted and the mixture is well combined. Transfer the mixture to a skillet.

3. Arrange the marshmallows, cut-side down, on top of the chocolate in the skillet. Cover the entire thing with marshmallows.

4. Broil for about 2 minutes, or until the marshmallows are golden brown (watch it carefully so it doesn't burn!).

5. Serve hot with the graham crackers for dipping.

Cast-iron tip: If you end up with a mess of hardened chocolate and sticky marshmallow in your skillet, don't panic! Hot water will usually be enough to melt it all away, but if there's still stuck-on mess left, fill the skillet with water and bring to a boil. Remove from the heat and let stand for a few minutes before pouring the water out, which will take all the residue with it.

Giant Chocolate Chip Cookie

Serves 8 / Prep time: **5 minutes** / Cook time: **25 minutes**

This giant chocolate chip cookie is so easy and fun to make. You can serve it as is, right out of the pan, or top the still-warm wedges with vanilla ice cream and a drizzle of hot fudge sauce for an extra special treat.

12 tablespoons (1½ sticks) unsalted butter, melted

1 cup packed brown sugar

½ cup granulated sugar

1 large egg

1½ teaspoons vanilla extract

2 cups all-purpose flour

1 teaspoon baking soda

½ teaspoon kosher salt

1 (12-ounce) package semisweet chocolate chips

1. Preheat the oven to 350°F.

2. In a bowl, stir together the butter, brown sugar, granulated sugar, egg, and vanilla. Add the flour, baking soda, and salt and stir or beat to combine. Stir in the chocolate chips.

3. Transfer the cookie dough to a skillet, pressing it to cover the entire bottom of the skillet in an even layer.

4. Bake for 20 to 25 minutes, or until the edges turn golden brown.

5. Cut into wedges and serve warm.

6. Store any leftovers at room temperature for up to a week.

Cast-iron tip: A 12-inch skillet is ideal, but you can use a smaller one if that is all you have. The baking time will have to be adjusted, because a thicker cookie will take about 5 to 8 minutes longer to bake.

Peach-Blueberry Crisp

Serves 4 / **Prep time: 5 minutes** / **Cook time: 25 minutes**

This is the quintessential summer dessert, full of juicy fruit and topped with a crispy, crunchy, sweet topping. If you're feeling decadent, top each serving with a scoop of vanilla ice cream. You can use any combination of fruit you like—try strawberries, blackberries, or nectarines.

2 cups fresh blueberries

1½ cups sliced peeled peaches

¼ cup granulated sugar

1 tablespoon cornstarch

1 tablespoon orange juice

1 cup old-fashioned oats

¼ cup all-purpose flour

¼ cup raw almonds, finely chopped

¼ cup packed dark brown sugar

¼ teaspoon fine sea salt

5 tablespoons cold unsalted butter, cut into small pieces

1. Preheat the oven to 375°F.

2. In a large bowl, combine the blueberries and peaches. Add the granulated sugar, cornstarch, and orange juice and toss to mix, coating the fruit with the mixture.

3. In a medium bowl, stir together the oats, flour, almonds, brown sugar, and salt. Add the butter. Using a fork, a pastry cutter, or your fingers, work the butter into the dry ingredients until the mixture clumps up into pea-size pieces.

4. Transfer the fruit mixture to a 12-inch skillet, spreading it out into an even layer. Sprinkle the oat mixture evenly over the top.

5. Bake for 20 to 25 minutes, or until the fruit filling bubbles and the top is crisp and golden brown.

6. Remove from the oven and let cool for a few minutes before serving warm.

Cast-iron tip: This recipe calls for a 12-inch skillet. You can use a smaller skillet, but the crisp may take a bit longer to bake.

Chocolate Dutch Baby

Serves **2 to 4** / Prep time: **5 minutes** / Cook time: **15 minutes**

Dutch babies are such fun because they puff up so dramatically while they cook. And they're as easy to make as a pancake. I love to top this chocolatey version with dollops of whipped cream and shaved chocolate. Or vanilla ice cream and hot fudge sauce. Or sliced bananas and caramel. The possibilities are endless!

3 large eggs

⅓ cup all-purpose flour

¼ cup sugar

3 tablespoons unsweetened cocoa powder

½ teaspoon kosher salt

½ teaspoon vanilla extract

½ cup whole milk

2 tablespoons unsalted butter

1. Place a skillet in the oven, and preheat the oven to 450°F.

2. In a medium bowl, whisk the eggs until they are frothy. Add the flour, sugar, cocoa powder, salt, and vanilla and whisk until smooth. While whisking continuously, add the milk in a steady stream.

3. Remove the skillet from the oven and put the butter in it. Swirl the butter around until it is fully melted and coats the skillet. Pour the batter into the skillet.

4. Return the skillet to the oven and bake for 10 to 12 minutes, or until the Dutch baby puffs up.

5. Remove from the oven and let stand for about 2 minutes before serving.

Brownie Skillet Cake

Serves 6 to 8 / Prep time: **5 minutes** / Cook time: **25 minutes**

This quick brownie cake is perfect when that chocolate craving hits. The semisweet chocolate chips punctuate the flavor with extra rich, gooey chocolatiness. Feel free to add 1 cup of chopped walnuts, if desired. I like to serve this cake still warm from the oven, topped with a scoop of vanilla bean ice cream.

8 tablespoons (1 stick) unsalted butter, melted, plus more for preparing the skillet

1 cup sugar

¼ cup unsweetened cocoa powder

2 teaspoons vanilla extract

¼ teaspoon kosher salt

3 large eggs, lightly beaten

1 cup all-purpose flour

1¼ cups semisweet chocolate chips

1. Preheat the oven to 350°F and lightly coat a 12-inch skillet with butter.

2. In a large bowl, combine the butter, sugar, cocoa powder, vanilla, and salt and stir to combine well. Stir in the eggs until fully incorporated. Add the flour and stir just until fully incorporated. Stir in the chocolate chips.

3. Transfer the batter to the prepared skillet.

4. Bake for about 25 minutes, or until the edges are dry and the center is just set. Serve warm.

Cast-iron tip: This cake bakes quickly because it is a thin layer of batter in a 12-inch skillet. You can use a smaller skillet, but you will need to adjust the baking time. Add 5 to 8 minutes if you are using a 10-inch skillet.

Measurement Conversions

Volume Equivalents	U.S. Standard	U.S. Standard (ounces)	Metric (approximate)
Liquid	2 tablespoons	1 fl. oz.	30 mL
	¼ cup	2 fl. oz.	60 mL
	½ cup	4 fl. oz.	120 mL
	1 cup	8 fl. oz.	240 mL
	1½ cups	12 fl. oz.	355 mL
	2 cups or 1 pint	16 fl. oz.	475 mL
	4 cups or 1 quart	32 fl. oz.	1 L
	1 gallon	128 fl. oz.	4 L
Dry	⅛ teaspoon		0.5 mL
	¼ teaspoon		1 mL
	½ teaspoon		2 mL
	¾ teaspoon		4 mL
	1 teaspoon		5 mL
	1 tablespoon		15 mL
	¼ cup		59 mL
	⅓ cup		79 mL
	½ cup		118 mL
	⅔ cup		156 mL
	¾ cup		177 mL
	1 cup		235 mL
	2 cups or 1 pint		475 mL
	3 cups		700 mL
	4 cups or 1 quart		1 L
	½ gallon		2 L
	1 gallon		4 L

Oven Temperatures

Fahrenheit	Celsius (approximate)
250°F	120°C
300°F	150°C
325°F	165°C
350°F	180°C
375°F	190°C
400°F	200°C
425°F	220°C
450°F	230°C

Weight Equivalents

U.S. Standard	Metric (approximate)
½ ounce	15 g
1 ounce	30 g
2 ounces	60 g
4 ounces	115 g
8 ounces	225 g
12 ounces	340 g
16 ounces or 1 pound	455 g

Index

Acknowledgments

As always, I am grateful to my husband and son for their constant support and insatiable appetites. I also wish to thank Annie Choi and the team at Callisto for their patience, expertise, and support in creating this cookbook.

About the Author

ROBIN DONOVAN is a cookbook author, recipe developer, and food blogger who loves her cast-iron skillets. She is the author of *Home Skillet* and several other bestselling cookbooks, including *Ramen for Beginners* and *Campfire Cuisine: Gourmet Recipes for the Great Outdoors*. From her home base in Berkeley, California, she blogs about easy international recipes for people who love food at AllWaysDelicious.com.